The Routes of English

4

by
Simon Elmes

Published by BBC Adult Learning
201 Wood Lane
London W12 7TS

Commissioning editor: Mina Patria
Additional material: Anne Barnes
Editor: Carol Stanley
Design: Anne McCarry
Picture research: Nick Pearson
CD producer: Neil George
CD replication: dBMasters, London
Printing: The Westdale Press Limited, Cardiff

ISBN: 1 86000 209 9

Cover picture: The Statue of Liberty in New York Harbour,
in a lithograph of 1886.

FOREWORD BY MELVYN BRAGG

Over the past two years or so, I've had the chance to explore the roots and routes of the spoken language of the United Kingdom, through a thousand years of its history. It's been an illuminating journey that has taken me and the Radio 4 production team from my home town of Wigton in Cumbria via the beaches of Hastings and the docks of Liverpool to the dialect-laden lands of Londonderry, Northumberland and Brixton.

Now we go abroad, lending an ear to the way English has developed beyond these shores, investigating not just the roots but the branches of English as they flourished and grew away from the main trunk of British English. Many took such firm root that they formed whole new trunks. So in America I was able to witness the whole process, from the uncanny re-creation of the language of the Pilgrim Fathers at Plymouth, Massachusetts, to the latest metamorphosis of American English that is 'Spanglish'.

The team travelled to Sydney, Melbourne and way into the bush to find out how Australian English is faring, on to Calcutta in India, and to South Africa to hear how English became the voice of freedom under apartheid. And in St Lucia in the Caribbean I listened as Nobel laureate Derek Walcott spoke lovingly about the local creole language and, historically, recast a section of his epic *Omeros* in it.

It has been a long journey, but one in which the vast diversity that English now represents has been tasted and reflected. And where next for the language, now spoken by more people as an acquired language than as a mother tongue? That too is a question for this enquiry as English is set to become a lingua franca for the world, and we address it in the final part of *The Routes of English*.

INTRODUCTION BY SIMON ELMES

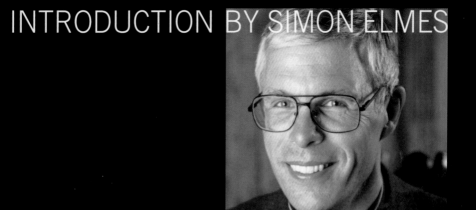

'I'm sorry,' I said, 'could you repeat that, please?' I was speaking to the large Texan at the wheel of my taxi in the state capital, Austin. I had been listening to him explain how he was going to get me to my hotel downtown. At least that's what I assumed – in fact, I hadn't understood a word. Not a single word. It was twenty years ago and my first encounter with American English on the ground, as it were. Maybe the problem was that I simply couldn't hear him above the sound of his revving clapped-out engine. Or that I was exhausted after the ten-hour flight. But I don't think so. The fact was that this variety of American English was unlike any that I had encountered previously. It was rough, ready, slangy and growled out through clenched teeth.

Of course, I soon got used to it, found my linguistic bearings, tuned in to the local vowel sequences and intonation patterns, and soon enough had gotten used to walking the sidewalk, making a left on the freeway downtown and using the crosswalk to get to the other side of the pavement. And like many millions before me, I found myself in both a strange linguistic land and at the same time an intensely familiar one, familiar from films and television and magazines.

So, it was no shock to see motels with 'parlors' and 'color' TV, though the finely-tuned linguistic antennae did home in on the 'Vacancy' sign outside (not 'Vacancies') that offered 'accommodations'. In fact I soon realised that almost every other word bespoke difference, like my driver's accent. I'd many times joked about the cliché about Britain and America being 'two countries divided by a common language', but I wasn't prepared for the reality. The surprise – even shock – is to me as vivid today as it was then. From that moment I became even more intensely fascinated by the ways in which the English language had become differently shaped beyond the shores of Britain. I wanted to know what had happened to this language, itself an import from continental Europe, the product of attrition and regional honing, soaker-up of great swathes of imported vocabulary, knocked into some sort of uniformity by printing – what, in short, had turned this English, that we have charted in three books and eighteen radio programmes, from something I knew and loved into something so different, so alien, so – well – un-English.

And so was born the spirit of enquiry that has informed the explorations made by Melvyn Bragg and producers Tony Phillips and myself of what Melvyn refers to as 'the branches of English' for this book and the final series of six BBC Radio programmes of *The Routes of English*. We wanted to follow the seed of English, carried by merchants and adventurers and planted often amid other languages on foreign soil. Why did it flourish there and eventually outgrow and overwhelm its rivals?

Trade took English overseas and, as we saw in our first book, brought great cargoes of words back to the British Isles. But while English consumed, absorbed and accommodated, the English we exported took root, and took over. It was a linguistic conquest that matched the human one – native American languages were rolled over as the peoples were slaughtered and overwhelmed: few of their words persist in contemporary American beyond the Mississippis and the Chappaquiddicks of the map. 'Squaw', 'teepee', 'lasso' ... it takes very little to line up the handful of regular native American terms that have gained universal currency within English. Likewise in Australia, the colonisation process produced small yields of Aboriginal words in modern antipodean English: 'boomerang', 'koala', 'corroboree', 'billabong' – these are hardly the backbones of the lexicon.

So does this mean that the story of the English linguistic diaspora is merely one of conquest, a litany of native peoples killed, or at best marginalised, their languages reduced to a paltry set of fauna and flora loan words in an overwhelmingly familiar lexicon? The fact is – as you will discover as you travel the English-speaking world through the pages of this book and the voices on the CDs – that what happens to English as it takes root on alien soil is a complex and far from uniform process.

Certainly, the colonial experience – almost always bloody in respect of indigenous races – has caused terrible linguistic losses along the way. But there are many more subtle processes at work too: processes of acculturation and absorption, of shifts of power within language and society, of incorporation and celebration. And these have shifted the ground a long way from the purely aggressive, dominating and overwhelming character of centuries past. Now English beyond the boundaries of Britain is far more influential than our local variety, and can count a far greater number of speakers with myriad accents and a host of local syntaxes, not to mention local lexicons comprising tens if not hundreds of thousands of words that have no roots back 'home' in Britain.

It is this story of huge shifts of linguistic power and influence that we wanted to tell through these pages. From the voices from 400 years ago of English pilgrims reaching for words to describe the brooks and valleys of the eastern seaboard of North America, to Captain James Cook and Joseph Banks hearing the first enunciation by indigenous Australians of 'kangaroo' in the last years of the eighteenth century. We were keen, too, to follow the ebb and flow of power as Afrikaans and English took root in the south of Africa, and to show how, in that tortured territory, each became so much more than simply a means of communication. We sought an explanation for the ubiquity and grace of the English used in India, and wanted to make landfall at the source of that rich Caribbean variety whose twenty-first century South London incarnation we so relished in part three of *The Routes of English*.

And for a final flourish, we thought we should try to encompass the notion of English as a world language, a global lingua franca for the new century, spoken often by men and women who have never lived in an 'English-speaking country', yet used – on the internet, in e-mails, in the forums where non-governmental organisations and international agencies meet and resolve differences and plan the future – ever more widely and more fluently.

Because, these days, English is the real asset to have. As a hand-painted poster high on a teetering gantry above the eastern Indian metropolis of Calcutta reminded me in its message advertising 'Spoking English classes': 'Ladies!! Get Going.'

contents

1

An American Affair

It is the signs that always hit me first: the sheer multiplicity of signs, of words, of instructions and announcements that greet you when you immerse yourself in an American landscape. America is a very wordy country; she loves her language and uses it at every opportunity to shout NAILS, LOANS, GUNS, LIQUOR at the passing throng. Where a discreet European pictogram instructs drivers to leave the carriageway with a quiet little arrow, its American counterpart shouts RIGHT LANE MUST TURN RIGHT. When walking down one of the great avenues in New York once, I recall the shock of encountering an American-accented command so strident that I imagined I could actually hear the rasping Brooklyn accent pronouncing it: DON'T BLOCK THE BOX! And I swear my imagination was not playing tricks over another shout from the kerbside, something along the lines of NO PARKING! NOT FIVE MINUTES, NOT FIFTY MINUTES, NOT... NEVER! American signs are vocal and slangy. And it is this characteristic vigour of the spoken language that has given American the dynamism to make huge inroads into well-established Englishes the world over.

In Britain, there is huge resistance to the wholesale adoption of American English – 'meet with', 'step change', 'protest' as a transitive verb ('protest human rights abuses'). Style books full of business jargon are routinely complained about in the press and on radio and television. Journalists, on the other hand, seem to be particularly keen to adopt vocabulary, expressions and even accents that perhaps are seen as hip – or at least different – simply because they are not home-grown. 'Leverage', pronounced in the American fashion to rhyme with 'beverage', has been heard on television, and not so long ago a British broadsheet journalist referred to having taken a 'hospital elevator'.

So what is it about American English that makes it so alluring? It would be foolish to ignore the power of global brands and the film and television industries to promote the American way with language alongside their attractive and desirable products. But there seems to me no doubt that the vividness that inspires so many US neologisms – 'carpet bombing', 'stretch limo', 'golden handcuffs', 'gridlock', 'gas-guzzler', 'downsizing', 'trailer trash', 'feeding frenzy' and thousands more – comes from a remarkable sense of linguistic freedom. In the United States there is no Académie Française to say no to 'no way', no snorting grammarians wielding Fowler's *Modern English Usage* in the face of a punchy phrase full of strong images and resonant rhyme. Granted, commentators in the US press and books regularly lament misusages and offer wise thoughts on socio-linguistic issues, but hot new words and phrases continue to pour out. And with an array of different language backgrounds contributing to the stream of American English, the sort of ground rules that govern the way many British people speak are often simply not relevant.

Yet the American language (as some now refer to it) sprang directly from British English. What were the influences that bore down on this transplanted English as it skidded off the main street and on to a track of its own? The playwright and thinker George Bernard Shaw famously described Britain and America as 'divided by a common language', and the differences we know about – 'sidewalk', 'gas', 'candy', 'drugstore' and the rest – are so well known as to be clichés. However, the subtle differences of expression that go far beyond such obvious examples (it's much safer to drive on the 'pavement' in America than in Britain, for instance) are telltales of the wholly different socio-linguistic climate that has governed America, compared with the UK.

3

John Cabot, navigator (1450–1498).

The discovery of America

Several people claim to have discovered America. During the fifteenth century people in Europe became aware that there were parts of the world which they knew nothing about, although they did not realise at first that their exploration would double the habitable world for their descendants. If they could find and explore this New World it might offer them great wealth and opportunity. There was therefore great rivalry between the major European powers, particularly England, Spain, Holland and Portugal, to equip ships capable of voyages of exploration and to find the best navigators to go on them.

The story of how English took root in North America and grew from being the mother tongue in the mouths of between 5 and 7 million Englishmen and women, to be the principal means of expression for 250 million Americans – and in many ways a model for the world – begins with the first settlement nearly four and a quarter centuries ago. The first expedition from England, led by John Cabot, set foot on North American soil in 1497, but it was a further eighty years before a party of English settlers first made landfall in America in the south of today's United States, in North Carolina on Roanoke Island. That first settlement of 1584, though, ended in disaster: the men and women had vanished without trace when a rescue party visited six years later.

The first permanent settlement – called Jamestown after King James I – was established a hundred or so miles north of Roanoke on Chesapeake Bay in 1607. But the most famous group of settlers were the first Puritans who, in November 1620, arrived in the *Mayflower*, landing 600 miles north of Jamestown on Cape Cod. The spot where they settled they subsequently named after the port they had left behind them, Plymouth. In those early days of the seventeenth century, the pattern of finding names for the new landscape was already well established – honouring the patrons and places from which they had come, and at the same time offering themselves a comforting reminder of home amid the alien and often threatening territory.

Today you can drive a few miles out of Plymouth, Massachusetts, and into a splendid reconstruction of that legendary home of the so-called Pilgrim Fathers at 'Plimoth Plantation'. Tumbling down a hillside, with a fort at the summit, a cluster of low

Perhaps the most famous was Christopher Columbus (1451–1506) who was born in Genoa but spent much of his life in Spain. In 1492 he persuaded King Ferdinand and Queen Isabella of Spain to sponsor an expedition which would sail westwards across the Atlantic and prove that the world was round. On his first journey he discovered some of the Caribbean islands, then on three further voyages reached the mainland of South America and the coast of Mexico.

At about the same time, Amerigo Vespucci, an Italian merchant and explorer who spent much of his time in the service of the King of Portugal, made several journeys to the New World and claimed to have been the first person to see the coast of South America.

Although it was not quite clear at the time exactly which part of the American continent he had discovered, it was nevertheless named after him.

Another Italian, Giovanni Caboto, better known as John Cabot, arrived at the mainland of North America in 1497. He and his son Sebastian sailed from Bristol, sent by King Henry VII of England with a patent empowering them 'to seek out, subdue and occupy at their own charges any regions which before had been unknown to all Christians'. They set out to discover more about Asia but instead found themselves on the edge of America. Further voyages of exploration led to the continent being gradually opened up to European colonisation.

cottages with thickly thatched roofs nestles amid woodland. The cottage walls are made from closely woven sticks, the muddy paddocks marked off with rough fences of upright palings and heavy, four-barred gates. These simple homesteads are dark and cool, with tiny openings for air and light. The atmosphere is filled with the crowing of cockerels. Men and women quietly bake bread and tend livestock, carrying pails and trundling barrows around the farm. Clad in simple skirts, breeches and the inevitable Puritan hats, these modern-day actors play a very convincing role as the inhabitants of the real Plymouth.

Outside the palisade – literally 'beyond the pale' – the Plimoth staff greet visitors with a cheery modern 'Hello'. Yet, once behind their rough fences, the twenty-first century re-enactors of the earliest Americans are unshakeable in their illusion of an English that they would have us believe is how their ancestors spoke nearly 400 years ago. Scott Attwood is the programme interpreter at Plimoth Plantation and he introduced Melvyn Bragg to **'Mistress Standish'** who was busily preparing to bake a batch of bread:

Welcome, welcome. Barbary is my name, I came over here 'bout four years ago now, into this place and living 'ere in this wilderness. I ain't so well acquainted with it yet, even though there are some things what I've become more acquainted with in the four years I've been 'ere. Butchering and slaughtering is one of them, something I ne'er had to do back in Ormskirk in Lancashire. In this place it is necessary.

The tones of 'Mistress Standish' are rounded and rural, with rhotic (pronounced) 'r's and unaspirated 'h's. Past participles have their '-ed' endings fully enunciated and the

Mayflower II, a full-scale reproduction built in Devon and sailed to its present berth in Plymouth, Massachusetts, in 1957.

vowel sound in words like 'roundhouse' is flattened and lengthened. 'Ocean' in the following passage also sounds quite different from today's word, pronounced much more like 'aw-ssian'. Melvyn Bragg wanted to know the circumstances that had brought 'Mistress Standish' to Plimoth:

You see, my 'oosbond, Captain Myles Standish, he was 'ere with a woman who was his wife, and she died. And so he sent a letter to me that I might come over 'ere and be his wife in her stead. And so I did. I come across. Well, first I tried to come across on a ship – oh, it was a terrible ship! Callèd *Paragon*. Aye, the ship was got not beyond the Thames River when it did cause itself to be so leaky that it 'ad to turn aboot and be repairèd. Then when that was repairèd it set sail again. About 'alfway across the ocean, there we were beset upon by such storms that would amaze you. This ended up blowing off the roundhouse on the fo'c'sle on the ship, and then they had to cut the main mast, t' keep the ship from going under. It was a wonder at all that we got ourselves back to London. But by then, they had built another ship to come across 'ere, a ship callèd *Little James*. I remember it well for it were a new ship and were set wi' such finenesses, and amazing it was to look upon. And so I got myself upon that ship. On another ship as well, what was 'ired out to come 'ere, bearing yet another must have been about three score people on that ship. Yet aboot two score upon the ship I was on.

'Mistress Standish' claims to be a Lancashire lass, which is quite feasible given that the settlers who formed the colony at Plymouth came from many corners of England. But the majority of them – and by 1640 they were a thriving and successful community of

The Pilgrim Fathers

In the early seventeenth century, religious discord and dissatisfaction with the Church of England drove many people to look for alternative ways of living. On 6 September 1620, 102 aspiring colonists set sail from Plymouth, Devon, in the Mayflower. Thirty-five were members of the English Separatist Church, the rest were servants or craftspeople.

The ship they sailed in was 90 feet long and 25 feet wide. She was not really big enough for that many passengers, and the fact that she was loaded up with furniture, provisions and livestock made the accommodation very overcrowded. The upper deck leaked badly and the passengers suffered terrible seasickness.

However, when they arrived at Cape Cod in November after 66 days at sea, only two people had died – and a baby, Oceanus, had been born. They now had to face the winter. As a contemporary said: 'They that know the winters of that country know them to be sharp and violent, and subject to cruel and fierce storms, dangerous to travel to known places, much more to search an unknown coast. Besides, what could they see but a hideous and desolate wilderness, full of wild beasts and wild men – and what multitudes there might be of them they knew not.'

The Pilgrims were weakened by the poor food on which they had survived during the voyage and they were unprepared for the conditions. By the end of the winter about half had died.

25,000 souls – were drawn from the east of England, especially Lincolnshire, Nottinghamshire, Essex, Kent and London, as well as some from the Midlands. Their dialects, while distinctive at a local level, will nonetheless have displayed a few common features that distinguished them from those, for example, of the south and west of England. Thus it was that the Plymouth colony tended to be 'non-rhotic' – they did not for the most part pronounce 'r' after vowels. Six hundred miles south, the Jamestown settlement in Virginia mainly drew its population from the English West Country, with its prominent 'r' sounds and rounded rural vowels, typified by the dialect of Somerset. And today, you can still hear echoes of these west of England roots in the so-called 'tidewater' accents of isolated Virginian island and valley communities such as that on Tangier Island in Chesapeake Bay.

Linguists have identified these two early versions of English dialect transplanted to the New World as the source of accent distinctions that today mark off the dialect areas of North America. The southern group, emerging from the Virginian settlements around Chesapeake, comprises broadly those states we often think of as the American South – Virginia, the Carolinas, Georgia, Alabama, Florida, Mississippi, Louisiana and southern Texas. In the middle lies the huge wedge-shaped mass of those states whose dialect area is known by linguists as 'Midland', fanning out from New Jersey and Delaware across the Midwest and embracing such far-flung states as Texas, California and Oregon. The northern band, with its roots firmly planted in Plymouth, Massachusetts, groups together New England, New York State, Michigan, Wisconsin, Minnesota, most of the Dakotas, Montana and Washington.

The Plimoth Plantation reconstruction is conceived as a snapshot of the community in 1627, just as the settlers began the process of fanning out up the coast and into the hinterland on that great journey that was to be the story of exploration and settlement in North America for the next 250 years. Melvyn Bragg asked **Scott Attwood** of Plimoth Plantation about the linguistic interaction with the native inhabitants of seventeenth-century Massachusetts.

I think their intent was that the English language would take over. They were very proud of being Englishmen. They had their differences with the reforms in the Church and other matters under the rule of King James, but they were still very proud to be Englishmen and considered it just the natural way that people should speak. There were much greater attempts to make the natives learn English than there were for anyone to learn the native tongues. In the second generation after the Pilgrims, Christian schools were set up for the natives to teach them English, with the simple presumption that this was a better way to speak.

It is above all the native place-names that survive into English rather than many general lexical items. Melvyn Bragg asked **Scott Attwood** to enlarge upon the linguistic relations between the Plymouth settlers and the native Americans.

Certainly many of the place-names around Massachusetts and other parts of New England – and, in fact, all of America – are lifted directly from native names. The native dialects seem to be almost as varied as English dialects at the time.

This area was called 'Patuxet' by the Pokanoket natives. It means 'little falling water' or 'a place of falling water'. There are natural springs here and that was really one of the

chief reasons the Pilgrims built here. 'Massachusetts' itself is a word that means 'great blue hills', for there are great grassy hills there that in certain lights get a bluish cast to them. Almost every place in New England has either an English name or a native name, whereas in other parts of America there are German, French, Spanish and Portuguese influences. Many of the town names and place-names here are translated specifically into English from what the natives would have called it – places with very simple sorts of names like Great Pond.

In about 1650 a man named Roger Williams, an Englishman who had been here, compiled what he calls a dictionary of the American language, by which he meant the native languages. He listed all the terms that he could find for animals and wildlife in the area – a lot of trade terms, for all the English were very interested in trading with the native people here. And his list doesn't have a lot of abstract terms but a lot of very concrete nouns and verbs – words for trees, rivers and places, for example. But as far as the sound of the native languages, everything that's written about them is certainly by Englishmen, because there is no written form of Pokanoket or Massachusett or any of the languages that existed here. So they were scribbled down phonetically and it is most likely there are mistakes within them.

The pioneers and adventurers who sailed from Britain to explore, trade, plunder and stake claims in new lands were all by definition neologists – coiners of new words – although they undoubtedly would not have recognised themselves as such. For the colonial British, whether in the New World or in Africa or Down Under, landfall and the establishment of a settlement meant meeting new things – plants, animals, people – close up. And that required a great deal of neologising.

The celebrated writer and journalist **Bill Bryson**, hilarious chronicler of life in Britain, Australia and New England, is also the author of a number of distinguished and highly readable accounts of the English language (notably *Made in America* and *Mother Tongue*). In New England, Melvyn Bragg asked Bryson how the first English settlers there had set about coining a suitable lexicon for the new colony.

Sometimes they had just to make up words for new items that were unknown and unfamiliar to them, generally by forming compounds, so you'd get things like 'bullfrog' for instance, and that happened a lot. Sometimes they would borrow words from the natives and that's how we got words like 'canoe', 'moccasin' and 'hammock' and so on. And thirdly, very often they would ask the native people what they called these things – unfamiliar things like persimmons for instance. And usually the words in the Indian languages were much more complicated and these things tended to get compacted in a way that made them more 'comfortable' in the English-speaking tongue. 'Hickory', for instance, was a word I can't even pronounce in the native original but it was something more like *'pahickeraw'* – a word that's sixteen or eighteen letters long in the native language becomes something like eight letters in English. That happened again and again.

In order, though, properly to be able to understand and interpret the native words, however mangled the version that eventually emerged into mainstream American English, the settlers needed an interpreter. The story of Tisquantum, or Squanto, a native of the Pawtuxet tribe, is familiar to American schoolchildren who learn early on about the vital role he played in the early days of the colony, and not merely as translator. **Bill Bryson** explained to Melvyn Bragg his own surprise on discovering just how remarkable the Squanto story was.

The native American languages of these coasts are incredibly agglomerate, difficult tongues, full of very difficult consonant combinations, and I always wondered how they managed to talk and teach it. But it turned out that Squanto had actually spent quite a lot of time in Europe. He had been effectively kidnapped by a fishing vessel which had taken him back and he had actually spent something like eight years mostly working in London, learning to speak English. Then he had come back to his homeland again to find that all of his relatives had been wiped out by smallpox. He was homeless and a virtual vagabond when suddenly the *Mayflower* pitches up, and here are some people that he knows and feels more comfortable with than even his own people now.

The Pilgrim Fathers were extremely fortunate to find a person who was both sympathetic and could communicate with them in an efficient manner. I mean you couldn't have had a more helpless group of people to start a new society. They brought all the wrong stuff, they didn't really bring people who were experts in things like agriculture or fishery. It was mostly a religious enterprise and they were coming with a lot of faith and not a great deal of preparation – so they were very nearly wiped out by the hardship of it, but with Squanto they just squeaked through. He taught them not only which things would grow but also how to fertilise corn seed by adding little pieces of fish – the fish would rot and actually fertilise the seed – and he taught them to eat all kinds of things from the seas. And thus, with his help, the English-speaking society eventually prevailed here.

However fragile that moment may have been, the subsequent story of first the American colony and, following independence in 1776, the United States, has been one of massive and constant expansion. The continent was vast and there was land to be had in great parcels, expropriated by the incomers from the indigenous occupiers.

There were great riches to be sought by, for example, the Gold Rush prospectors, obscure creeks and gulches to be mutated by some transforming discovery from a huddle of wagons into a cluster of homesteads, which became a town and then was dubbed a city. Tuba City in Arizona is one such, a sprawl of shacks and shops stretched out with little apparent sense of plan around a road junction, and as unlikely a 'city' in the British sense of the word as any place in North America. Yet again when it comes to building this new nation, new notions of what things *are* are required.

When an English word like 'city' is uprooted and applied to something quite different, somehow the word changes with the meaning. The letters on the page may be the same, but the 'cityness' of a British city is gone. Likewise a 'creek', as found all over America, is not what British people know as a creek (a sea inlet) but a stream or small river. 'Streams', on the other hand, so familiar a feature of the British landscape, both physical and linguistic, barely figure in America. Thus, interesting things happen to words when the scenery gets shifted around them. Suddenly everything is different: context is all.

All this is without taking account of the many other linguistic influences that came to bear on North America in its 400 years of European colonisation. During the massive expansion, shiploads of new immigrants from other parts of England and, in the eighteenth century, from Northern Ireland took their chance across the Atlantic. Fifty thousand Irish and Scots-Irish also arrived during the early years of that century, to form a total American population in the newly independent nation, as calculated by the first census-takers of 1790, of approximately 4 million.

Other European languages, too, were to be heard on American soil. Spaniards were occupying parts of the south and west of America, the French had left indelible influences in the north and in Louisiana, and New Amsterdam was only to become New York as the Dutch influence there faded. Germans, too, came in large numbers to Pennsylvania at the end of the 1600s, while 100,000 Africans had reached the southern states as slaves by 1775. Further huge waves of immigrants flooded across the Atlantic in Victorian times, the Irish fleeing famine, Germans and Italians the consequences of unsuccessful revolution. They were joined in the 1880s by persecuted Jews from Central Europe, and so great was the desire to seek a new life that, during the early years of the twentieth century, 750,000 men, women and children were sailing up the Hudson River every year to become Americans.

Every new community brought a fresh linguistic pressure to bear on the now thoroughly deracinated English of old England. **Bill Bryson** told Melvyn Bragg of his own experiences of this cultural and linguistic ferment.

The pattern in the nineteenth century was for people from a particular speech community to come and live together, just to transplant themselves wholesale. And my father, who was born in 1915, could clearly remember, in the little area of south-east Iowa where he grew up, communities where people had spoken Swedish exclusively, and other communities where they'd speak in Danish exclusively, and other communities still where they'd spoken German exclusively. And that was well into the twentieth century. But today those places have become pretty well wiped out. You can go to places like that and you will still find German names or Dutch names or whatever in abundance, but ask them to say a few words of Dutch or German and they can't, they've forgotten completely.

Immigration into America

As the United States of America began to be a great industrial power, immigrants arrived from all over the world. Between the Battle of Waterloo in 1815 and the outbreak of the First World War about 35 million people entered the US, totally altering the nature of its society and culture. The rural economy all over Europe was changing and people came from Sweden, Norway and Germany, Greece, Sicily, Italy and, most significantly, Ireland where the potato famine had deprived many of their livelihood. Some were refugees, like the Jews fleeing the pogroms in Russia; others, in a variety of situations, sought a more liberal society.

Whatever their reasons, the immigrants arrived in thousands, mostly in New York. They looked up at the Statue of Liberty and read America's promise to comfort 'your tired, your poor, your huddled masses yearning to breathe free' and must have felt hope. Many were already ill from the voyage, some were sent back because they could not pass the medical examination they had to undergo in the huge warehouse building on Ellis Island. But those who were lucky prospered enough to become confident Americans.

So in the cliché 'melting pot' of America, English emerges as the ultimate flavour of the stew, whatever the original national linguistic ingredients, and with no variation from coast to coast. Or so the wisdom used to go.

Travel by air across the vastness of the United States, from New York in the east, say, to San Francisco on the west coast, and you cross huge physical boundaries – the lumpy hills of New York State, the horizon-stretching flatness of the Midwest with its endless straight highways seemingly ruled across the landscape, the snowy jagged peaks of the Rockies and the fertile vinelands of California. The sheer overwhelming diversity of the continent of America is laid before your eyes. Do the trip in the other orientation, from rainy Seattle in the north, for example, down to baking San Antonio, Texas, and again the territory morphs through a dozen different realities before your eyes. Difference, contrast: this is the reality of the United States. Americans are used to it. Such vast changes of environment are something that Europeans are less likely to encounter when travelling within the boundaries of their countries.

On the other hand, what Europeans do find customary is linguistic diversity. It is nothing for a European to travel 50 kilometres and be confronted with not only a different accent, but a different language. For the average American, however, until relatively recently, to travel from one end of the country to the other was to encounter people who spoke the same English and in more or less the same way. Certainly, there were broad differences of accent from north to south, but the differences (what linguists term 'regional variation') were small. Now though, as **William Labov**, Professor

of Linguistics at the University of Pennsylvania in Philadelphia, explained to Melvyn Bragg, pronunciation is on the move.

We have never had the very intense dialect differentiation found in Britain. What we have is a series of older dialects in the east and the formation of new regional dialect boundaries in the west, but you could travel through large areas and see very little difference, in fact until recently people thought that America is almost undifferentiated compared to the United Kingdom. But the second half of the twentieth century brought a radically different situation and we now have an intense differentiation of American dialects, but not on a small local scale – on a vast regional scale: around the middle of the twentieth century, people in the Great Lakes area started to change their vowels.

It is difficult to illustrate these sound changes in print, and readers are recommended to listen to the quotations from Professor Labov's research recordings on the accompanying CD. However, the following examples give some idea of this latterday Great Vowel Shift currently taking place within American English.

It's rotating vowels, where it begins with 'sacks' becoming 'sex', then 'socks' gets to be like 'sacks', and 'sex' becomes like 'sucks'. 'Buses' becomes like 'bosses' and finally 'bosses' gets down like 'buses'.

This change was dubbed the Northern City Shift.

The cities involved are Syracuse, Rochester, Buffalo, Detroit, Toledo, Cleveland, Grand Rapids, Flinton, Gary, Chicago, Madison, Milwaukee – all those great cities around the

Great Lakes. In fact, if you think about the history of the Athenian Empire, it was defined by the cities around the corn routes of the Aegean, and this is like that. It's all those great cities around the Great Lakes.

We didn't know originally that this change was so general. Now the linguistic atlas of the United States is completed we can tell you that it is a characteristic of a large region of about 88,000 square miles, about 35 million people all moving in the same direction – who don't know it because this is quite unconscious.

But **Bill Labov** enters a major limiting factor to the scale of the changes:

African Americans don't participate in them at all – not in the least. In every single major city that we found throughout the country these sound changes are characteristic of the white population.

Labov attributes the fact that the communities' linguistic behaviour is affected in different ways to what he calls 'residential segregation' – white and black Americans tend not to live in the same housing areas of cities. But if the Northern City Shift is exclusively a white phenomenon, that is not to say that African American English is static. It too has developed a number of new characteristics over the past fifty years.

The feature that's best known is the use of 'be' meaning 'habitual': 'He'd be running his mouth', 'They'll always be telling me this.' And we have an exponential growth in the young black population of the use of this 'be' meaning 'this is what habitually happens': 'If he be here he'd be doing this', meaning 'It's because he's doing it all the time' as opposed to 'He's here right now.'

And there are many other features of African American English that are new. The most

striking is the use of 'they done', which you don't hear on mass media or in TV sitcoms, but it's used in the following way: 'They done drunk up all the wine by the time you get there.' That means 'They will have drunk up all the wine.' Now if that was all there was to it it would be a simple translation of 'will have'. But people also say to someone 'I'd be done kill that man if he mess with my child again.' In this case, that cannot mean 'I will have killed him', it means something else. It means that this event will follow absolutely certainly from the second event.

In recent years, one of the other significant features of the way language functions in the United States has been the rise of what is known as 'Spanglish'. Spanish, traditionally a major linguistic influence in the south-western states is now set to become the largest minority language in the whole country. In fact, in a number of US cities the numbers of Spanish speakers are approaching or have already overtaken those with American English as their first language. The Latino effect is here to stay.

With such a deep well of influence, it is little surprise that a lingua franca has developed to help bridge the divide and give expression – within the context of English-speaking culture – to the life of Hispanic America. On the streets of Spanish Harlem in New York you hear this 'halfway house' of Spanglish loud and clear every day. And a short subway ride away at the heart of Manhattan on Times Square, flanked by the ever-flashing messages (in English) of the neons, lie the offices of *Latina*, a women's magazine for the Spanish-speaking community. **Betty Cortina**, the Editorial Director, explained to producer Tony Phillips that her readers were 'bilingual and bicultural'.

[They are] women who live in between, in the sort of cultural nexus where many of us were either born here or raised in this country, and yet we still feel a very strong traditional

pull from our families, from our heritage. And so we have one foot firmly planted in each of two cultures.

Cortina's case is typical: her parents were Cubans who emigrated in the 1960s and Betty was born and raised in the United States, though 'very much in the Cuban tradition'. As a result, she speaks fluent English and Spanish.

Many Latinos in this country either grew up with fluent Spanish being spoken at home or somehow the din of Spanish in the background. For a very long time I came to work and I spoke English and now I speak a little bit of both at work. When I went home I spoke Spanish and ate a different menu of foods than any of my friends did and had a totally different culture happening at home and a different experience happening at home. My parents struggled very much to keep our traditions and our culture alive and yet still prepare me for life in America where the culture was different and the expectations were different.

Latina reflects this biculturalism, weaving Spanish words into articles in English with ease and providing précis translations in Spanish.

It's the way we talk, and as journalists we've all been trained to write this way. When we go to church we find ourselves praying in Spanish and then we go to work and we find ourselves speaking in English quite naturally, and so sometimes there is a difference. I mean, the Spanish for me in particular tends to be the language of my spirit and so when I pray I pray in Spanish, and then I work in English. Or if you're a mum, when you get angry you yell at kids in Spanish because that's the language that you discipline children with. So to ignore that emotional component in the language is just unrealistic.

Professor Anna Celia Zentella teaches at New York's City University and she has made a close study of how Spanglish operates. She endorses Betty Cortina's positive view of the way Hispanic speakers use their bilingualism to mix up their means of self-expression – to do what we have identified so often in these books and in many different linguistic contexts around the world: to code-switch.

Spanglish now is for some of the young people who actually embrace those practices a very positive way of saying 'I belong to both of these worlds, I have a foot in both of them, I can manage well in both of them.' For the first generation, the people who were born and raised in Latin America, it's still a very negative term and they don't want to think that they have Spanglish speakers in their midst. But that word is also reflective of a new transformation in the culture.

And it is far from being a random mélange: Zentella's research has shown the same techniques at work across the US.

There's a skill to it – it's not a hodge-podge or a mish-mash. You don't suddenly decide to jump in and out in any spot, it's very carefully orchestrated. I liken it to knowing how to follow a salsa dance partner that you've never met before and being able to take off and not step on each other's feet. People who are bilinguals converse doing the same kinds of grammatical moves in and out of both languages that are very complex linguistic moves. You just can't switch anywhere but just at particular points in the sentence.

The tendency is to switch at clause level, so that a sentence like 'I really need to go down town because I have to buy my mother a present before her birthday on Sunday', you would switch at the parts of the sentence where Spanish and English have very similar syntactic structures. So it's as if you were the conductor [driver] of a train and you were changing tracks – you have to know what both the Spanish linguistic track is grammatically and what the English grammar allows, and then switch at the points in which the Spanish grammar and the English grammar converge. You might say 'I really need to go down town, *para comprar* something for my mother *antes de* her birthday on Friday.'

In another example of what I would include under the bilingual practices of code-switching, you have a sentence that is entirely in Spanish, but that is in fact made up of 'Spanished' English words. So that if I say 'Los teenagers están jangueando en el rufo en vez del jol', what I'm saying is 'The teenagers are hanging out on the roof instead of the hall', and I have 'Spanished' a number of the nouns there, but the grammar of the verbs and the agreement is all in Spanish structure.

Speaking from his New Hampshire fastness, writer **Bill Bryson** sees novel linguistic features like Spanglish as merely dots on the horizon – it is a phenomenon that barely impinges, and certainly not day to day. His view of it is in consequence both more measured and less fearful.

People have expressed great alarm because there are so many Spanish-speaking people in the country and they feel as if Southern California will become a Spanish-speaking domain. I think that's ridiculous myself. It certainly is not supported by historical events. Most people come here voluntarily, they want to be part of the wider society, take part in it fully. They want to watch American TV programmes, not just the couple of Spanish-language stations they've got. There's every incentive for people to speak English in this country.

What happens is that there is a great pool of Spanish-speaking people, but that pool is constantly being renewed and replenished. As people from that Spanish-speaking pool

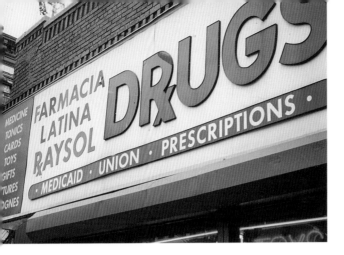

have become monolingual in English, they're being replaced by fresh input from other Spanish-speaking countries. So that it seems as if this pool is large and growing as indeed it is, but it isn't static, it's constant, there's a constant turnover of people.

Far more significant is the internationalism of American English.

There's so much more closeness, and anything, a word or an attractive slang term that arises in New York City today can be in London tomorrow or even this afternoon. I mean, there's just so much more contact. The world is becoming increasingly one place.

One world, one culture, one language? It is a theme we shall return to in the last chapter of this book. Yet I believe that for all the cultural and linguistic crossovers – the baseball-hatted teenagers, the shared worldwide TV culture (I have seen versions of *Who Wants to Be a Millionaire?* in Singapore, Sydney, Connecticut and Calcutta) – and the power of the global pop and computer markets, it will take far more than a bit of borrowed language and some envied cultural artefacts to homogenise the world. **Bill Bryson** is less sanguine:

I think the danger is not in the future that British-speaking people won't be able to understand American people, but rather that there'll be nothing to separate them, that you won't be able to recognise a British person as distinct from an American person, and that we will somehow meet in the middle. I think that would be a terrible shame. I think it's the differences that give the language so much of its charm and make it so attractive.

Somehow, though, I just cannot envisage any official in charge of Britain's thoroughfares ever countenancing the erection of a sign on a British high street shouting at motorists DON'T BLOCK THE BOX. Can you?

2

Indian English

From Raj to Regeneration

Another hot dawn is breaking over the city of Calcutta. Against the eastern sky a silhouetted line of palms is mirrored by a lake of stagnant water. Under a tree, a huddle of prone bodies lie asleep, uncovered to the stifling, humid night. Half-light conceals the true distress of these people, of their lives played out amid the detritus on the pavement, in the gutter. On the other side of town, in a trim brick house, Kushal Biswas is stirring. It is no cooler for him and his nieces, but their house has glazed windows, a slowly turning fan to churn the heavy air around a little, television, a telephone and a lavatory. When he makes me tea, Kushal can turn on a tap for water.

On the table in Kushal's home is a copy of *The Times of India*, and talk soon turns to the latest opinion poll figures for today's vital state elections. The conversation – like the newspaper – is in English. Fluent, beautifully cadenced, meticulously grammatical English, full of subtle vocabulary and accurate yet fluid construction. Kushal is a DJ with All India Radio, and he talks equally comfortably about boy bands and thrash metal and points of English syntax. This is early morning tea taken with a member of the privileged 5 per cent of Indians for whom English is a natural means of expression. And Kushal Biswas is as fluent in English as he is in his native Bengali.

India is, of course, an unequal place. And the all too visible contrasts between those who have something (often not much by Western standards) at one extreme and those who are off the bottom of the scale at the other are still reinforced and delineated by linguistic boundaries. Although 200 million Indians are said to have some grasp of the English language, 95 per cent of the population has no real working knowledge of it. And yet, wherever you go in Calcutta, English is at least as prominent a feature as Bengali (the local indigenous language) or Hindi (the favoured national tongue). The

24

posters for today's election are all at least bilingual in Bengali and English. Buses carry signs declaring them to be 'ON ELECTION DUTY'. Bus stops are clearly marked 'Bus stop'. A shop sign announces: 'Junction 96 – Your friendly Internet parlour'. And, despite the local authority's attempts to change the name, Shakespeare Sarani is still almost always referred to as Shakespeare Road.

Changes to the names of cities have known greater success, so travellers today find themselves heading for Mumbai, not Bombay, Pune where once it was Poona, and Kolkata rather than Calcutta. This indigenisation of the spelling reflects a truer transcription of the local pronunciation, but it is not without its political loading. In fact, in India it is virtually impossible to speak of English without reference to the colonial history that goes along with it, to the catalogue of wrongs dealt out by the British to their subject people during the Raj.

But despite its colonial associations English remains omnipresent, a uniting force that lies outside the rivalries and tensions generated by the indigenous languages. And with an interwoven history that goes back more than four centuries, beyond the creation of the English East India Company in 1600, many Indians feel the English language is as much an expression of the Indian soul as Bengali, Hindi, Gujarati or Kashmiri.

The distinguished young novelist **Amit Chaudhuri** was born in Calcutta and, although brought up speaking Bengali, writes his books in English. He tried to pick his way through the tangled linguistic relationships in his native city.

I think English has played a double role. Yes, it has been a language of unification. It has also been the language through which people in India became more self-conscious, and therefore conscious of their own differences – from each other, from the English; so it has

25

played this dual role. The English themselves mustn't take too much credit for it because they didn't know this was happening. It's entirely to the credit of the Indians that they used this in this way. In modern Indian history English has been very much at the heart of things. It's a lingua franca but it's also more than that, it's a part of the growth of the indigenous languages and the modern forms as well. So it has also unconsciously been a part of that self-expression of difference – of different identities – which is also very vital to what India is.

But as a Bombay-educated, Calcutta-born writer, how does Chaudhuri feel about the 'Indianisation' of his cities?

I think the renaming of streets is bad – it's really an irrelevant thing to do, and I feel the renaming of Calcutta as Kolkata is really ridiculous, personally. But then again it just signifies a different phase in Calcutta's history, where it has ceased to be that renaissance city which was 'Calcutta' and now has become another city which is 'Kolkata'.

But the street names, even in Bombay, are often referred to by their old names – I mean, no one refers to Flora Fountain by its new name in Bombay for instance. And here I think the old street names are very much part of oral memory, of cultural memory, and they are referred to even by people who don't know of this particular history. People like taxi drivers who are maybe just migrants who've come in from a neighbouring state about two years ago – they still refer for example to Dalhousie Square [named by the British for the victims of an insurrection against them, and since renamed for the insurgents as Benoy Badal Dinesh Bagh, or 'BBD Bagh' for short].

Yet how can you erase history? That's the one thing you can't do and it's the most dangerous route to take ever, I think. When people try to turn the clock back or try to change history or erase it, I think that that's a form of violence. It may be an overt form of violence or just a violence done to your past or whatever your memory. It is a form of violence and I think it's better avoided. You can't change your history. Although I think that the fact that these cities are being renamed is because they have now gradually become different cities. 'Mumbai' is a different city from 'Bombay', where I grew up, and 'Kolkata' I think is a different city from 'Calcutta'. I do believe that.

What is undeniably true is that despite all the posters and signboards in some form of English, the vast majority of the city's 12 million population only have the tiniest smattering of English words. And as for the thousands living lives of illiterate and irredeemable destitution in the slums near the railway station and along the airport road, they are completely disenfranchised by the ubiquity of English. **Professor Sukanta Chaudhuri** teaches English at Jadavpur University in Calcutta. He is a trim, fast-speaking, meticulous user of English with a ready wit. He knows his English as well as he knows his Calcutta, of which he is the author of perhaps the most admired and exhaustive portrait, entitled *Calcutta, the Living City*. He recognises the riches that the country and he personally possess in using English as a means of expression, but ...

At the same time, there is a great sector in the life of the common Indian where English is being imposed on him at the moment, artificially. It is artificial and wrong and counterproductive that road signs and destination boards in Calcutta should be written in

Indian English

English is spoken in many different ways in India. There are pidgin dialects and there is a standard English which is spoken with a slightly different intonation from elsewhere. There are different grammatical constructions and a vocabulary derived from Indian languages or adapted from English words or phrases. Often in India you will hear people say 'I am understanding' instead of 'I understand' or 'Is he knowing the answer?' Or you will hear words joined together to make a new word as in 'cousin-sister' or 'key-bunch'.

Many Indian words have become familiar in English. Words like 'bungalow', 'verandah', 'calico', 'chintz' and 'jodhpurs' all originated in India, as did 'pukka' meaning smart, and 'posh', which is said to derive from 'Port Out, Starboard Home' – the instruction given to ships' booking clerks by rich people who required cabins on the shady side of the boat as they travelled between India and England.

English. That is not natural. It is natural to a small group of the urban élite who speak in English. It is not natural to the people around them and outside their doors to use English for these purposes.

And Professor Chaudhuri favours the renaming of Calcutta's streets and squares, so long as it is done pragmatically.

The problem is that many of these new names are much too long and clumsy to be used. If they were shorter and more practicable, snappier, then people would use more of them. In fact a few names which are shorter have come into common use. For example, nobody says Lansdowne Road any more, they say Sarat Bose Road, but the new name for Dalhousie Square – Benoy Badal Dinesh Bagh – is such a mouthful that nobody uses it.

As for Kolkata and Calcutta, I personally still refer to my city as Calcutta. But then again I seem to disagree with the majority of my English-speaking compatriots in thinking that there's nothing basically wrong with this move. That is after all how we pronounce the name of our city in our own language, so where's the harm? It's still sufficiently close to the old name.

But there is too much English around in this country, in all kinds of grass-roots contexts – at the level of public services, public notifications – so that a very large section of our population, who only speak, read and write their mother tongue, are effectively disenfranchised in their own country. Signboards, official forms, even destination boards on public transport, road signs, shop signs – a very large proportion of these are in English. And English alone more often than not. Or, if there is a translation into an Indian language, the translation still follows the structure of the English so closely that it is unintelligible unless you also understand English.

So at the level of public facilities and services, public announcements, yes, I am strongly opposed to the use of English. There is of course the other argument that in a country this size, where so many people have to live in or travel in parts of the country whose language they don't speak, one does need some kind of lingua franca, and English provides that lingua franca. But there are also many contexts where this argument does not apply, where the application is purely local, and there I think we have positively to take steps to rid ourselves of English.

The story of how the language took root in the subcontinent is bound up intimately with the history of Calcutta itself. Trade with India had been formalised in 1600 with the establishment of the English East India Company, but English sailors had obviously visited in search of goods to trade and bring back to Europe well before then, as the eminent **Professor Raja Ram Mehrotra** of Banaras University told me.

The first Englishman who landed in India was an ambassador sent by King Alfred the Great, way back in 884 AD. And he brought with him some gifts from the King for the tomb of St Thomas. Well that's the solitary instance of its time, but the continued connection with England, with English people, began in 1579, and to be more precise October 1579 – an Englishman called Thomas Stephen, who landed in Goa. And Father Stephen played a significant role in inducting British merchants to the various parts of the country. And it was on 31 December 1600 that Queen Elizabeth I granted a charter to a group of British traders to carry on business in India.

With the establishment of the East India Company's first permanent trading station at Surat in 1612 and the opening of further outposts in Calcutta, Madras and Bombay by the end of the century, contact between English speakers and the indigenous

Dates in Indian history

1526 The Mogul Muslim dynasty invaded. Their rule lasted until the end of the eighteenth century, although it was losing power by the middle of that century. The Mogul emperors erected fine buildings, developed a strong administration and encouraged religious harmony between Hindus and Muslims. They were also influential in laying the foundations of Indo-Muslim art.

1600 The East India Company was chartered to promote English trade in spices, tea, cotton and other products. The French and Dutch set up similar companies.

1757 Robert Clive of India outmanoeuvred the French who were competing for supremacy in India and defeated the ruler of Bengal at Plassey, clearing the way for a great expansion of English trade.

1857 The Indian Mutiny brought about the transference of control of India from the East India Company to the British Government.

1885 The Indian National Congress was founded.

1925 Mahatma Gandhi became president of the Indian National Congress and began campaigning for independence.

inhabitants of south Asia became regular and intense. Language, as well as goods, became an article of trade. During the next hundred years the British overcame the power of other European nations in the subcontinent, with a notable victory over the French at the Battle of Plassey, not far from Calcutta, in 1757. **Professor Mehotra:**

After the arrival of the traders, there were two groups of Englishmen who influenced and encouraged the use of English in India. One was the Army and the other was evangelists. The missionaries started working in India in the year 1614, becoming very active by the year 1659. They started education, opening schools and colleges. Most of the missionaries came from northern England and Scotland, and so in the eighteenth and nineteenth centuries most of the English educators or those who were in charge of education and English studies in India were from Scotland – and very few from southern England. And so they exercised tremendous influence on the English speech of people in India. Some of the most famous colleges in India were started by Scots, like Christchurch College in Madras.

Meanwhile, the strength of the Mughal emperors waned as the influence of the East India Company waxed, such that in 1765 the Company took over the collection and administration of taxes and revenues in Bengal, in the east of the subcontinent, and British sovereignty over India began. Following the Indian Mutiny of 1857–8 the powers held by the East India Company were subsumed by the Crown.

The British established their capital in what had originally been a group of three small villages, of which one – Kolkata – gave its name to the new settlement. Today, the architectural legacy of Calcutta, capital of the Raj, forms the solid brick and stone heart of the modern city. The occasional modern block and the sprawl of post-colonial low-rise construction bear no comparison with the big-boned buildings around BBD Bagh, the former Dalhousie Square. Here are the Writers' Building, where clerks or writers laboured in their thousands, and the General Post Office. Not far away is the Victoria Memorial Hall, a cream-puff extravaganza built, so they say, in an attempt to rival the splendour of the Taj Mahal. And nearby St Paul's Cathedral (Calcutta), the headquarters of the Anglican church in the region, possesses a slim neo-Gothic tower in gleaming white stone that would not look out of place in Oxford or Cambridge.

Education as a mission and the thirst for learning lie at the heart of the deeply ingrained consciousness of the English language in India. **Professor Mehrotra:**

The first school which was started in India for the teaching of English was in a suburb in Calcutta, and the first textbook, the first English book to have been published in India, was titled *The Tutor, or, A New English and Bengalee Work Well Adapted to Teach the Natives English*. It was prepared by John Miller and published in Serampore, dated 1797.

In 1835 the role of the English language in British India was forever changed by a memorandum, known archaically as a 'Minute' and written by the distinguished essayist and future author of the legendary *History of England*, Thomas (later Lord) Macaulay. As a member of the Supreme Council of India, he proposed the establishment of an English educational system. Macaulay's Minute on Indian Education states: *'I think it clear ... that we ought to employ [our funds] in teaching what is best worth knowing; that English is better worth knowing than Sanscrit or Arabic; that the natives are desirous to be taught English, and are not desirous to be*

taught Sanscrit or Arabic; ... that it is possible to make natives of this country thoroughly good English scholars ...'

Macaulay's pronouncement was controversial at the time and still arouses great annoyance, hatred even, today. Yet it was material in framing the linguistic and intellectual destiny of a whole nation.

Another of the great Raj buildings of Calcutta still stands as a living memorial to that powerful educational impetus that flourished under British rule. Behind a wall, on a street where cars and brilliant yellow taxis clog the roadway and the pavements are lined with hundreds of bookstalls blockaded by tangles of browsing students, stands Presidency College. Founded as Hindu College in 1817, it has for nearly 200 years been a hub of learning in English to Calcuttans. **Dr Samita Sen** now teaches History and Women's Studies at Calcutta University, but was once a student at the College. She took me through the ancient gates and away from the hubbub into the courtyard. Three cool storeys of arcaded corridors lead away into classrooms, the dark, grand staircase plastered with posters and noticeboards recording examination results.

Hindu College was founded in the early nineteenth century, jointly by some leading Indian, Bengali citizens at that time, and the British. The first most famous teacher was Derozio, Henry Vivian Derozio, who first attracted young Bengali students to Western philosophy, and started what was called the Young Bengal Movement – the first generation of rationalists who rejected Indian religions, superstitions, values. You see, Indians realised that a proper knowledge of the English language was going to be critical to their access to

Lord George Curzon (seated, centre) was the youngest ever viceroy of India (1898–1905). He loved the pomp and ceremony of the office, but also had a sense of mission toward the Indian people.

The British Raj

When Robert Clive gained control of Bengal in 1757 on behalf of the East India Company, Calcutta became the centre of government. A large army was built up and civil servants were employed to collect taxes and conduct the administration. A hundred years later the absurdity of a huge country being run by a trading company became clear. Following the Indian Mutiny (1857–8) the British Government took over and the British Raj was born.

In 1877 Queen Victoria was proclaimed Empress of India and soon viceroys were appointed to rule in her name with enormous pomp. India, and especially Calcutta, suddenly became posh. Young men at a loss for a career would join the Indian army and spend much of their time enjoying the social life of the viceregal court or playing polo. Young girls would be sent out from England to find a husband. Many of them married and lived pleasantly idle lives waited on by Indian servants. Cocooned in a little English world of their own, they were so convinced they were of a superior race that few of them ever really made contact with Indian people or Indian culture. For some it was a paradise of parties, gossip and leisurely days in the sun, but for others it was lonely, unhealthy and frightening, as the English graveyard at Calcutta pathetically demonstrates.

government resources, to jobs, to all kinds of changes that were happening in Calcutta city at that time, so there was a great deal of initiative from the Bengali middle class. There was also obviously an interest on the side of the government and the East India Company at that time, because they needed to use Indians in commercial and government administrative purposes, and they needed better means of communication.

Not surprisingly, given the educational tradition in which they have been schooled, Dr Samita Sen, Amit Chaudhuri, Sukanta Chaudhuri – and DJ Kushal Biswas – all have remarkable English. But they, like many I met during my visit to Calcutta, also displayed a remarkable level of intellectual analysis. **Kushal Biswas** offered the following insight into the way he and his contemporaries speak.

If you heard me speaking in Bangla, then you would find that I was as fluent in Bangla as in English, but that's not something surprising, is it? I have been born and brought up in a Bengali household. But I think it's important to realise in households like ours – and there are many of them definitely in the educated middle class in Calcutta – there are a lot of people who use both languages equally and they are familiar with both. I mean, when I speak to a Bengali friend of mine – and he needn't be a teacher of English – I could conduct an entire conversation in Bengali, or I might conduct an entire conversation in English, or I might mix the two and speak to him in either mainly English interspersed with Bengali words or Bengali with a smattering of English terms. And there is no logical sort of choice made, and neither I nor this friend of mine would have any problem. I can't say that this applies to everybody but it does to a lot of the middle class in Bengal.

Many middle-class Bengalis aspire to what they refer to as an 'English-medium' education for their offspring. Whether English is the natural medium of expression in the household or merely a useful second language giving access to power via the legal and administration systems of the country, the schools that offer a formal training in ideas, articulated through the English language, are a powerful force in the upper echelons of Indian society. For all the desire in government circles to democratise and indigenise the language of the country, English simply keeps bouncing back. I visited one such 'English-medium' school.

La Martiniere College was, paradoxically, originally a French foundation. Major Claude Martin grew up in Lyon, France, in the first half of the eighteenth century, but spent much the greater part of his life in India where, after defending the French cause, he eventually joined the East India Company in whose service he amassed a fabulous fortune. This wealth he endowed to the foundation of schools in Calcutta, Lucknow and his native Lyon. La Martiniere College, Calcutta – I visited the girls' school – is another fine, white-painted colonial edifice, with colonnaded portico and children clad in neat school uniforms, 'Prefect' and 'House Captain' badges pinned to their blouses. The sixth-form girls of La Martiniere were staggering, not simply in their outstanding command of English (for many not their first language), but also in the way they eagerly engaged with ideas. Here is a sample:

Girl 1: English is our main means of communication. I mean we rarely converse in Hindi – maybe sometimes at home. In school the main language we converse in with our friends is

English. With families it's different perhaps, and it's very essential to know your roots, your regional language, because if you want to actually work in India, and if you want to reach out to the people, you must know the regional language, because that is very important. At the same time you must know English because that's how you're going to communicate with people of your level, and maybe at the international level. So both are very important in their own way.

Girl 2: That's something good England has given us, because it's the common language which all of India uses.

Girl 3: If you're talking about India then Hindi I think would be the main binding language, but all over the world English is the one binding language.

Girl 2: Like you said, for regional languages, if you have to converse with the Indians, the middle-class Indians, I think Hindi will be the language, because that is the language we converse in with illiterate people, with everyone. But if you're talking about people from abroad, English is the only language which is common between us, and that's how we can communicate to the world.

Noticing that several of the girls were wearing badges for Macaulay House, I asked these brilliant 17 year olds how today's generation of English users viewed Thomas Macaulay's observations of 1835.

Girl 1: He said that a single shelf of books, European books, is better than all the books of Arabia and India and Asia. It actually sums up what he really thought about India, so that makes him evil for us.

Girl 2: I think it is great, what we have, our literary tradition. I mean, you can't sum it up in one word or one line, it's truly great, it's more than 5,000 years old.

Girl 3: I feel that, OK, there were definitely negative aspects of the British Raj – that's why we struggled to break free from them – but whatever positive aspects there were we definitely imbibed them and are gaining from them even today.

Girl 2: And before the British Raj actually existed we have so much of history much before that, and that is so amazing. I think we really don't need to push away the British Raj because we are what we are today.

Girl 3: It's part of our culture.

And so, indeed, it is. Downtown, in the slightly seedy corner of central Calcutta known as the New Market, where you pick a difficult path between the pavement traders and the busy shopping traffic, Domino's Pizza has its Calcutta outlet. Here is ultra cool for young Calcuttans, all as happy to chat away in English as to use the internet café next door and the video games saloon – when the regular power cuts permit, of course. And they watch satellite television, where cricket is served up to passionate viewers in their millions, wrapped in the international packaging of a slew of English-speaking star commentators who are known throughout the world. For cricket-mad India one size fits all, and it is English-speaking. **Kushal Biswas**:

Geoffrey Boycott has really opened our eyes. He's a very popular TV commentator among all these young people whenever cricket happens in this part of the world. So you find people who used to imitate the way a famous cricketer walked or the way he used to wear his cap perhaps, and you have people who imitate the way Boycott talks. And it's wonderful, you know – ''E's not a bud butsman,' with a Yorkshire accent. We find it greatly amusing. I mean, I find this kind of English very attractive. A lot of people would

not associate an Englishman with this kind of English, but I dare say it's just that we haven't had too many BBC programmes using this kind of English.

Likewise, the rolling election programme on TV – full of exit polls and very sophisticated analysis of the day's ballot in the important state vote – is mainly run in English. But not entirely. When one speaker on the panel of experts replies in Hindi to a question posed in English, no one turns a hair, but the debate flows on for a few minutes in Hindi. It then reverts, quite seamlessly, to English. And as for *Who Wants to Be a Millionaire?*, Indian fashion, the questions and the potential answers are given in English, while the discussion and the agonising over whether to 'phone a friend' is conducted in Hindi. There must be few places on this earth where bi- or rather multi-lingualism is today so institutionalised. **Kushal Biswas** mixes the languages up when he broadcasts.

At one time I used to feel personally that this wasn't really a good use of either English or Bengali, or for that matter Hindi. But it is the way we do speak nowadays – I mean you do have people who, even when they're not on air, do mix English and Bengali all the time, and they're using this kind of mixture as freely and as unselfconsciously as they would be doing any one of these individual languages. So it's great fun and it is really creative.

In fact, Kushal told me that at his (English-medium) school he used to spend whole afternoons with a friend punning across from English to Bengali, a tactic now adopted, he points out, in the current crop of advertisements from Coca-Cola.

But if television, cricket and Coke are pushing fragments of contemporary English further out into the mass audience, the vast majority of Indians still have no notion of English and are lost when confronted by it. **Professor Raja Ram Mehrotra**, though, has made a study of these more marginal applications of the language amongst social groups well outside the educated élite, and has found forms of very limited English used with surprising levels of possible communication.

I spoke to a group of people – hawkers, boatmen, astrologers, snake-charmers, pedlars, small traders, music players and priests of various categories – and the important thing about the users of pidgin English in India is that they are not educated. They haven't learned English formally or in any other way. They have picked it up through interaction. And they are very well able to communicate, in their respective domains, in English.

To give you just one example: a trader wants to explain to a prospective buyer, someone from England, 'Buy this sari – don't go to the other shop, don't buy it elsewhere, this may be bad quality.' What he actually says is: 'Some sari bad quality – country go, wash, colour finish.' Now mark the last sentence: 'Country go, wash, colour finish.' In effect: 'When you go back to your country, and wash this sari after you use it, the colour will vanish.' Look at the brevity – a small number of words that try to convey the meaning, and the context makes it clear. Their stock of English words is just 250 to 300. And with this small inventory, this small stock of words, they are able to communicate, convey their meanings.

Despite these efforts by the linguistically unempowered, **Professor Sukanta Chaudhuri** is adamant that the way English is still used in contemporary India and the way it underpins so much that is significant in people's lives – governance, administration and the law, for example – is a positive disadvantage.

The upper courts and certain of the business of the lower courts is still transacted in English. And with general official procedure, there again, the common Indian has to go to somebody who knows English to get a letter interpreted, or to write a letter in turn, all too often. These days of course he can usually use his own language, but only up to a point. Furthermore it's often expressed in the kind of officialese that I believe actually has been obsolete in Britain for the last fifty years. You still get a lot of letters beginning with things like 'I beg to submit that …' or 'I pray to submit that …', and things like 'The undersigned is directed to state …' – which of course means nothing.

In the lobby of the Taj Bengal Hotel, under the seven clocks indicating the time across the world, the exquisitely beautiful receptionist coolly asks whether the professor requires a taxi home. They are both Bengalis; they speak not Bengali, but English. Outside, beyond the razor wire and barking loudspeakers and guards keeping undesirables out of the hotel compound, an elderly man is being shaved under a tree. Another is weighing grain in a hand-held balance, while a third swills a grimy used glass in filthy brown water. In the middle of the pavement sits a wrinkled old man, utterly naked, possessionless, a stream of piss meandering from him to the gutter. The brilliant red and white signboard opposite, hand-painted in hesitant capitals, urges: 'LADIES!! GET GOING. SPOKING ENGLISH CLASSES. LEARN SOCIAL GRACES'.

3

English in the Caribbean

The Hurricane Speaks

It was the Barbadian poet Edward Kamau Brathwaite who wrote: 'The hurricane does not roar in pentameters.' By which he meant that the natural voice of the Caribbean was far removed from the formality of Old World vocabulary and syntax. He would, he vowed, use a language which truly reflected the life of the islands and not that of a small village in the English Midlands four and a half centuries ago. But a poet's preference for the vernacular of his own people and experiences rather than the language of Shakespeare is only one aspect of the long and involved history of Caribbean English. In fact, the story of language in that looping scroll of islands strung across the map over a thousand miles is one of the most complex in the world.

It is truly astonishing that we can write at the beginning of this book of the broad uniformities of American varieties of English, while within relatively short sailing distances to the south of Florida, the Caribbean islands display a degree of variation and a richness of vocabulary, pronunciation and syntax – not to mention a diversity of linguistic origins – seen in few other places in the English-speaking world. Another glance at that map of the Caribbean, however, begins to show why.

Though the landmass of North America is vast, it is continuous. Settlement took place in broadly a westward direction from the first landfalls on the eastern seaboard. The islands of the Caribbean, on the other hand, are just that – islands. And as we know from our own British island, language functions differently there. Communication can be more difficult and less frequent, and though the Caribbean islands display common features, of lifestyle as well as of language, it is a fact that Jamaica is as different from Trinidad as it is from Barbados, to name but three parts of this huge archipelago. After all, two hundred or so miles of ocean separate Trinidad and Barbados, and a further thousand miles (as well as dozens of other inhabited islands) lie between Barbados and Jamaica.

We should, then, on the contrary, note how astonishing it is that communities so distant from each other should display so many common characteristics, not least the distinctive and broadly homogeneous pattern of prosody (the sound of the spoken language).

As with all the stories we tell in this book, the history of the English language in these diverse islands is one of importation and cultural adaptation. It is also very much not simply the history of the English language, but of the Spanish, the French and the Dutch, as a result of the colonial ambition that prompted the great European maritime explorer powers to seek bounty and territory across the globe.

The Spanish came early to the Caribbean, thanks to Christopher Columbus, and by 1517 they had already initiated the practice of slavery there. The conquerors were merciless to the indigenous peoples such as the Arawak and Carib – as the old joke goes, the Spaniards came ashore and fell on their knees and then on the natives. The indigenous population was virtually wiped out.

As the Pilgrim Fathers far to the north were beginning to construct the American dream in the 1620s, other British adventurers were arriving on the islands of St Kitts and Barbados in the Caribbean. They brought their troops and their culture – and their servants. And, according to **Dr Hubert Devenish** of the Department of Language, Linguistics and Philosophy of the University of the West Indies in Jamaica, it was not long before the first African slave labour arrived on the islands.

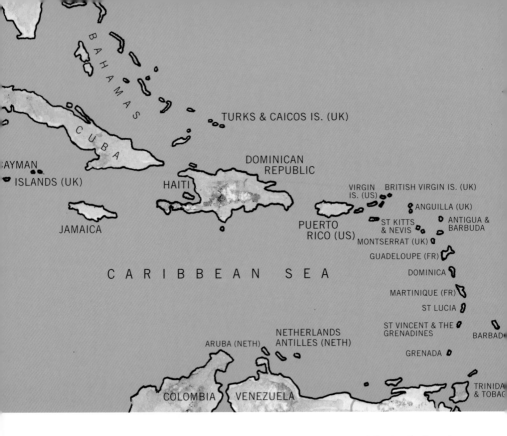

The people who arrived in the first instance were, apart from the original colonists, large numbers of indentured servants, who were in a sense the first servile population in the Caribbean, of British origin at least. A lot of the research suggests that they came from the West of England – Devon, Dorset – as well as from Ireland. And it seems that many of them were Irish Gaelic speakers, but as well speakers of Irish English. But what happened in the Caribbean is that somewhere around 1650, or the late 1640s, Africans started to replace English indentured servants as the servile population. This coincided with the growth in sugar – the discovery that sugar was a major commercial export commodity. They established with the sugar plantations the need for large numbers of labourers and so the Africans started coming in in about 1648 or thereabouts.

The seventeenth century was dominated in the Caribbean by the so-called 'triangular trade' in goods, sugar and African slave labour. Ships sailed from ports such as Liverpool to Africa where, in exchange for cheap goods, they took on a cargo of slaves who were shipped to the islands of the Caribbean where they were put to work on the sugar plantations. The third leg of the voyage was the carriage of sugar cane back to Europe for refining.

Early settlement in the Caribbean

When Columbus sailed west in 1492 he expected to reach Asia but instead found the Caribbean islands which then became known as the West Indies. He went on to discover the South American mainland and the coast of Mexico. The Spaniards who had paid for his voyages soon colonised large parts of the mainland and some of the larger islands such as Cuba, Hispaniola (Haiti and the Dominican Republic) and Puerto Rico. The smaller islands, inhabited mostly by Arawaks or Caribs, remained more or less undisturbed until the English and French (and the Dutch and Danish in some cases) began to realise the need to have a presence in that part of the world.

The islands have slightly different histories but the basic pattern is the same. The Europeans drove out most of the native peoples, established plantations and brought in slaves from Africa. When the plantations were no longer profitable they were abandoned and the islands left in varying conditions of insecurity which sometimes led to unrest. Many islands are now independent; others still belong to the UK, USA, France or the Netherlands.

The English speaking islands include:

Jamaica – settled by the Spanish in 1509, captured by the British in 1655, independent since 1962.

The Bahamas – settled by British from Bermuda in 1648, became a British colony in 1717, independent since 1973; only about 30 of the 700 islands are inhabited.

Virgin Islands – roughly a hundred islands: settled by Britain and Denmark in the 17th century, the Danes sold their islands to the US in 1917.

Dominica – fought over by the French and the British, became a British colony in 1805, independent since 1978.

St Lucia – settled by the French in 1650, ceded to Britain in 1814, independent since 1979.

St Vincent & the Grenadines – disputed by France and Britain in the 18th century, ceded to Britain in 1783, independent since 1979.

Grenada – colonised by France in 1650, ceded to Britain in 1763, independent since 1974.

Barbados – settled by the British in 1627, independent since 1966.

Trinidad & Tobago – settled by Spain in 1532, became British in 1802, independent since 1962.

It is hard to image the barbarous conditions on board the rat-infested, stinking ships where slaves had to survive (hundreds did not) for months, tossed by storms, roasted by tropical heat – and attempting to make themselves understood. It was the policy of the slave traders to draw their cargoes from tribes with mutually incomprehensible language backgrounds in order to minimise the risk of them planning rebellion and seizure. Thus communication between the slaves from different areas, as well as with the mariners, was severely limited.

A widely held theory suggests that, as a result, some form of basic English developed on board in order to enable at least minimal contact. Many of the seamen on the slave ships spoke English, and their cargo of men and women needed somehow to make themselves understood to them – and to each other. However, **Peter Roberts**, Head of Linguistics at the University of the West Indies in Barbados, maintains that any meaningful contact in the conditions that reigned aboard the slavers was an impossibility.

They were crammed together. It was a matter of trying to get as many people into the ship as possible, so it is doubtful that there would have been much interaction between the

slaves. Even though the middle passage was long – it took months – the amount of interaction would have been minimal, and conditions really didn't provide for a lot of interaction because a lot of the slaves got sick, some of them died, and the health conditions were very poor. So you can't imagine anything like a 'bedroom' situation where people are interacting and are joking – that's not what happened.

However, when the slaves reached the islands, interaction was more feasible and this is how it is believed the first Caribbean pidgins arose. A 'pidgin' is what linguists call a 'contact language': a primitive means of communication that arises where no common linguistic forms exist, of limited vocabulary and restricted grammar, and used only for a restricted range of functions, usually to do with trade.

From the very limited expressive range of these pidgins have sprung, in communities in the Caribbean and in many other parts of the world, what are known as 'creoles'. Professor David Crystal, in his definitive *Cambridge Encyclopaedia of the English Language*, describes a creole as 'a pidgin language that has become the mother tongue of a community'. In an environment such as that of the imported African slaves in the plantations of the Caribbean, with their diverse tribal and linguistic origins, Crystal observes: '… increasing numbers begin to use a pidgin as their principal means of communication. This causes a major expansion of the grammar and vocabulary, and of the range of situations in which the language comes to be used.' As generation succeeds generation, these pidgins become fully-fledged languages, or creoles, which, while owing much to the original base language (including French, Spanish and Portuguese as well as English), have developed a distinctive identity of their own.

To experience the riches of this creole linguistic environment, Melvyn Bragg went to

visit the great writer and poet of the Caribbean, **Derek Walcott**, Nobel Prize-winner for his epic work *Omeros*. At his home on the island of St Lucia, Walcott expressed his own relish for the range of expression that the creole he speaks affords him as a writer – as well as the more formal standard English which still has an important status among the population of the islands.

I think I'm lucky in the fact that I have two languages, both of which are natural to me. In other words I don't think of English as a different language to creole, nor do I think of creole as something inferior to English. So I'm lucky. I do not think in creole in order to be able to write, but if I'm doing a play, or parts of a poem, that need creole, or parts that have to express themselves in creole, then I have to think in creole. I think in English and write in English, and if one has to have a priority or choice in terms of which language it is, I'd be reluctant to say it was English, but the fact is that I do think in English and write in English.

The reality is that I was brought up talking English, which wasn't strange – my mother was a teacher – and I lived in a context of English, right through from the time I went to

primary school, through college, to the university. Plus in St Lucia there really are dual languages – both French creole and English.

As Derek Walcott implies, the language of the English-speaking islands of the Caribbean has both a formal form, which in many respects resembles standard British English – or, increasingly, standard American English – and a local creole variety. **Dr Hubert Devenish** of the University of the West Indies in Jamaica:

There are two relatively distinct language varieties that you can call English in the Caribbean. There is standard Caribbean English, which is something like what I am talking to you, and then there's another variety, that is quite distinct, and those are what are called by linguists English-lexicon creole languages.

In fact, Professor David Crystal goes much further, claiming six varieties 'of varying distinctiveness' for the area. 'The situation is unique', he writes, 'within the English-speaking world, because of the way the history of the region has brought together two dimensions of variation: a regional dimension, from which it is possible to establish a speaker's geographical origins, and an ethnic dimension in which the choice of language conveys social and nationalistic identity.'

The Routes of English producer Tony Phillips and presenter Melvyn Bragg with poet Derek Walcott.

Alongside the creoles and a form of standard British or American English, Crystal identifies, for example, local varieties of this standard reflecting such island influences as past colonial contact (French, Dutch, Spanish and so on) and local Amerindian languages. He also observes that there is an emerging form of educated English, spanning the thousand or more miles between the islands, which is known as Standard West Indian English. So in this complex linguistic landscape, the notion of 'Caribbean English', implying a single identifiable form, is far too simplistic.

As we indicated earlier, many theses have been advanced to explain the development of the creoles of the Caribbean, notably that of the contact languages or pidgins that grew up amongst the African slaves. But there are other persuasive explanations. According to **Hubert Devenish**, the scholar Derek Bickerton is the leading advocate of this traditional view.

The key thing is children are born in that situation. Human beings need language in order to survive, communicate with each other. Children are born in the situation where there's a whole massive complicated language input, all kinds of things happening, and the children say 'Oh, I don't have reasonable tools to learn here, I will have to make language all over again.' And so they go back to the basics – the information about tense and so on. So that you will get in all of the creole languages, whether they be French creole or English creole, the information about time. So maybe 'I walk' means something like 'I had walked'; 'had been' – 'I'm a been walk.'

Bickerton develops a complex analysis of how these creoles deal with time and tense, using basic English terms but a syntax that owes nothing to the standard language.

He says this system isn't copied from English, and is not even a system in his view copied from West African languages. This is something that is part of a natural human predisposition to speak the language, and when you don't get, or have no exposure to a single language that is properly structured and so on, you make up a language of your own, and it will always be structurally the same wherever you go.

An opposing view of the source of these creoles is expressed by a rival scholar, Mervyn Alleyne, who maintains that the sorts of tense construction typical of these languages can be sourced to a common underlying West African language grouping.

What you've got is a process of linguistic acculturation, where, even though West African languages are very different from each other, they belong to a big language family called Niger-Congo, and there are certain key features which they share in common. And one of those features, Alleyne argued, is this tendency to put markers before the verbs in the way that I have just described. And what Alleyne argued is, given a common exposure to English, they then tended to borrow the forms from English, but used them in a structure which was essentially West African. And that is why, for example, Caribbean creole languages have no inflections for pronoun forms. So 'Me go' would be 'I am going', and 'Tell me' – 'They told me'; 'This me book' – 'This is my book.' So there's no inflection in the form of 'I', 'me', 'my'; and the same would go for 'you', etcetera.

Devenish cites another case:

'Me run go school' would be translated in English as 'I ran to school.' The 'go' is the directional marker telling you where you're running to, whereas the English form has a preposition and the 'go' form, which is a straightforward verb, like 'Me go there' would mean 'I went there.' But in this particular context – 'Me run go school' – 'go' would have the effect of a preposition. And you could get other forms such as 'He run come here', meaning 'He ran here' or 'He ran in this direction.' So 'go' and 'come', which are perfectly normal verbs in and of themselves, end up in those sentences representing directional prepositions, meaning 'to' and 'from'.

Using these examples, **Hubert Devenish** describes how the two theses of creole development interpret them. According to the 'back to basics' principle:

These children who grew up in a situation where they didn't have a proper language input didn't therefore get exposed to prepositions in English, did what was a linguistically natural thing which was to take verbs and use them for prepositional values.

Now the opposing camp says 'Rubbish!' West African languages are amongst the few groups of languages that have serial verb constructions of the sort that I have just outlined, and when you look at languages like Yoruba, Edo, Igbo and so on, they have structures which parallel that.

It is impossible in this short survey to do justice to the diversity and individual character of the islands' linguistic stories. One such, that gives a notion of just how many strands of language and history are woven into the linguistic fabric, comes from Barbados where the indentured servants who arrived with the British colonists brought a lexicon of regional, notably West Country English, to the island. **Peter Roberts** of the University of the West Indies identifies them in modern Barbadian speech.

You have words like 'frowzy' – a word that is very common in Barbados. You have words like 'ramboat', and 'nose-hole'. And when you look at these words, these are not words that developed in Barbados. They come from regions of Britain. 'Frowzy' refers to a person who doesn't smell too good or that doesn't seem to bathe very often, and is wearing the same clothes all the time – 'frowzy'. But this is a British regional word, it came from Britain, it's not a word that was created in the Caribbean.

And Roberts makes an interesting comparison between Barbados and Jamaica, where the landscape of language was shaped by a different rhythm of development.

Barbadian English is much closer to standard English than Jamaican or Trinidadian or that of any of the other islands, and the reason for this is that, if you compare Barbados with Jamaica, both islands were British for the same length of time. But remember that Jamaica was Spanish before it became English, and during the period of slavery in Jamaica the Jamaican planters preferred to replenish the population by importation of Africans, which meant that if you keep on importing Africans into the situation, you're reinforcing African language within Jamaica. In the case of Barbados, the importation of Africans declined as the slavery period went on, and as the planters depended more on natural increase, at the end of the slave period the majority of slaves in Barbados were creole slaves, and a slave born in Barbados, whereas that was not so in Jamaica. So that is one of the reasons that Barbados is different.

Back on the neighbouring island of St Lucia, poet and writer **Derek Walcott**'s experience is – as for many educated West Indians – of a diverse linguistic universe, with English as the official medium of expression and creole as the day-to-day language. In St Lucia, it is a French-derived creole.

There was never a moment in which I thought of English as being a strange language or different or an inherited language even. The language we spoke at home – my mother being a teacher – was English, and the language that the servants spoke, and which my mother would speak to the servants in, was the French creole. And there was a language of the street, which is a French creole. But the education that one had was very much modelled on an English public school education.

The excitement of creole did not come in a literary way for me until much later when I began to listen to some of the folk songs that are there in creole, which are beautiful, not just as melody but also as lyrics. And I didn't have that instinct to write in French creole, in patois, until much later.

When Melvyn Bragg asked Walcott to recite a section of his epic work *Omeros* for the tape, he found himself at the heart of a moment of linguistic ferment, rethinking and recasting a section of dialogue in the local St Lucian French creole.

He said 'belle lune'. Now when I hear that, that's terrific. 'Nice moonlight' and 'belle lune' – oh my God, you know, I didn't do it because I'm a coward – no, not really! I didn't do it because I didn't think of it. But when I look at it now and you say 'belle lune', which would be the French *belle*, it's French creole. 'Nice moonlight', the moonlight is *la lune*. There's something richer in a sense for hearing that. I'm not regretting it, I'm just saying that when I have done it, what I have felt when I was doing it is to feel that same delight in writing the French creole as in English and perhaps even a little more.

In Jamaica, at the western extremity of the arc of the West Indian island chain, the poet **Joan Andrea Hutchinson** testifies to an equal degree of passion about and commitment to the way Jamaicans use language. For her and the young people she teaches, the ability to express herself not only in Standard West Indian English but also in the local island creole in Jamaica affords her an advantage.

We've been told for many years that this area is not good enough – our language, our food, the way we dress, the way we look. So we've gone through a lot of processes of altering ourselves, altering the way we look, the way we eat, the way we dress, the way we speak, because we've been told for years it's not good enough. And too many people, for example, have felt that the Jamaican language is only to be used for entertainment, and I say 'Absolutely no.' I do a lot of motivational speaking in schools and I work with a lot of teenagers, and what I find is, because a lot of them use the Jamaican language, when I go into a classroom to talk with teenagers, if somebody else comes in and speaks in standard English for the whole time there's a kind of alienating factor that is there. Now when I walk in and I talk in a mixture, because I can switch easily – when I switch easily from creole, from Jamaican, to the English language, the students are more comfortable with me.

Code-switching from one form of language to another, cross-fertilisation between cultures, histories and different colonial backgrounds, not to mention the influences from America and other Caribbean islands – these are modern phenomena that are part of the daily experience of language in the islands. In Barbados, physically far removed from Jamaica, the influence of that island's powerful culture and language is today being felt. **Peter Roberts** of the University of the West Indies in Barbados.

For example in Jamaica, if you wanted to say 'I am eating' you would say 'Me a eat', which is a different structure altogether. People of forty and over in Barbados would never say

'Me a eat', but some of the young people would use this kind of phraseology now, this kind of structure, and among themselves they understand what it means. And if you look also at some of the expressions that the entertainers use, these things also will be understood by the young people. It is part of a whole culture that has become a Caribbean culture, I think in the same way that you get in Britain among children of Caribbean parents. They don't have to be of Jamaican parents, but they can produce a kind of Jamaican English because they see it as a mark of identity. So this Jamaican influence is becoming much stronger, even in the Caribbean.

So there may be some features which are beginning to emerge as Caribbean rather than specific to particular island cultures and creoles. Yet there is one aspect of Caribbean English which nonetheless unites the speech of the whole region: what linguists know as the prosody of the language – its accentuation and tonality. The overwhelming feature of Caribbean prosody is its stress pattern, which, unlike standard British or American English, is what is known as 'syllable-timed'. That is to say, the stress is more or less equal for all syllables – as opposed to 'stress-timed' varieties like British English where a stress on one syllable affects the meaning and function of a word. So the word 'Jamaica' receives in Caribbean English approximately equal weight on each of its three vowel sounds, whereas British English gives particular stress to the second syllable.

The result of this syllable-timing is to alter the value of some of the core sounds of English, such that the 'schwa' or unstressed vowel sound, like the 'a' in 'ago', is virtually non-existent. To the ear accustomed to meaning being expressed through individual rather than even stress (as in British or American English), the vocalic values

HATS OFF TO KITCH

A CD by Lord Kitchener, the legendary Caribbean calypso artist from Trinidad & Tobago, whose trademark was satirical or political lyrics blended with a steel pan drum accompaniment.

Caribbean music

When the slaves worked in the plantations they were often forbidden by their masters to talk to each other. Instead they chanted to a tom-tom rhythm, telling their news and commenting on what was going on around them in a patois which only they really understood. These songs were often accompanied by folk dances. A type of song which developed in this way was the calypso. When slavery ended and the West Indian community gained its independence the tradition of calypso singing remained and became popular in Europe.

that result from varying the emphasis away from the standard can prove tough to decifer and, at the extreme, misleading.

So in what ways are the Englishes of the Caribbean changing to meet the needs of evolving tastes and cultures? We have seen the central role that Jamaican creole is assuming, so what of new lexical elements? **Dr Hubert Devenish**:

All languages expand to deal with what they have to deal with, and so the same happens in Jamaica. You get borrowings from English, but borrowings from English very often with a culturally quite distinct meaning. The classic example that comes immediately to mind is 'deportee' where a 'deportee' in Jamaica refers to a second-hand motor car that has been imported, usually from Japan. And so they say 'A lot of people are driving a deportee.'

And **Richard Allsopp**, who is a former academic at the University of the West Indies and now Director of the Caribbean Lexicography Project, continuing work begun on the *Dictionary of Caribbean English Usage*, offers some other examples of Caribbean linguistic 'hijacking'.

When a Bajan [Barbadian] speaks of somebody being 'malicious', they do not mean what the English word 'malicious' means in the English dictionary or English society – they don't mean 'spiteful and vindictive', they don't mean that at all. It's very serious. They mean 'nosy' or 'poking your nose into', 'inquisitive' – that's what 'malicious' means. 'Oh she's too damn malicious, she wants to know everything. Another example, a very famous one for me, is 'trouble'. 'Don't trouble the book', 'Don't trouble my bicycle', meaning 'Don't interfere with' something or someone. 'Don't trouble the women's children', 'Don't

The modern version of the calypso has a relaxed rhythm and loose phrasing which can be adapted as it goes along. It often consists of racy comment on current events, political scandal or sporting occasions and is sung to the accompaniment of a steel band. When West Indians left the Caribbean to work in Europe, they took this form of music with them. It was particularly popular in the fifties in England and is now most commonly heard at carnivals. It has had considerable influence on the way in which English is spoken in the West Indian community in the major cities of the United Kingdom and has kept alive the sorts of rhythms and phrasing now sometimes referred to as Black English.

Another major influence on the way people speak is the Jamaican popular song and dance form called reggae which is usually associated with the Rastafarian religion. The original reggae songs were in Jamaican creole and focused on issues of poverty and unemployment and the idea of return to Ethiopia which the Rastafarians regard as their homeland. The music became increasingly complex and successful in America. Bob Marley, particularly, helped to spread its popularity.

interfere with the children.' 'Trouble' is a very old sense of, I would say, Elizabethan poetic usage as in 'the wind troubled the waters'. But not for us. 'Trouble' is a general word for 'interfere with'. Generally speaking you would hardly find Bajans and eastern Caribbeans or even any part of the Caribbean speaking or using 'interfere' in this sense.

Back to **Hubert Devenish**:

And the language is continually growing. The example that immediately comes to mind is the going word 'chi-chi man', because 'chi-chi man' is a term for a homosexual, a male homosexual. But that came in or at least I became aware of the word and its meaning only as a result of a very popular song, that's really still quite popular, this *Chi-Chi Man* song. And I'm assured by my informants that the word wasn't around eight months ago.

With vocal and influential Caribbean speakers, writers and musicians overseas from London to New York and further afield, the awareness of Caribbean varieties of English has never been greater. The music business lies close to the heart of this expansion, but the less strident yet every bit as influential and powerful voices of an Edward Brathwaite or a Derek Walcott ensure that the complex riches of the Englishes of the island chain of the Caribbean Sea are gaining both a currency and a status undreamed of by their forebears. Nobel laureate **Derek Walcott**:

We have that duality that can go on in a language, and for me it's very fertilising, it's very enriching, because you can have a third language in which you can combine the two languages and make something out of them privately as a writer.

4

Australian English

Badge of a Nation

Right: Celebrations in Bathurst in May 2001 to mark the centenary of the federation of Australia. The local historical re-enactment society re-create the early days of New South Wales: the man in the tricorn hat is playing the part of the celebrated Governor Lachlan Macquarie.

It's a cool autumn day at the showground in Bathurst. Heavy clouds stream across the early May sky, but the sun when it does appear still has the power to coax flies into buzzing annoyance around the hundreds of men, women and children flooding towards the barn-like structure of the showground halls. This is rural New South Wales, 150 miles almost due west of Sydney's skyscraper-edged harbour. But it could be a different world, because this is what Australians still call 'the bush'. Not, they point out, the real bush – that's 'out west' – but still rural enough to justify the term.

The crowds are here to mark the centenary of Australia's federation as a nation in 1891, when the six states came together to form one country, the Commonwealth of Australia. It was a moment that marked the start of a process of national self-assertion and proud independence that today is almost completely accomplished. Only the head of the sovereign on the coinage and an occasional half-hearted rendering of *God Save the Queen* mark the formality of the – dwindling – links with Britain. It is *Advance Australia Fair* that gets the crowds going, and *Waltzing Matilda* (yes, still) that puts a swing in the step of the marching band.

The story of the English language in Australia is inextricably bound up with this march of history from federation, via such landmarks as the raft of legislation passed by the Gough Whitlam governments of the 1970s, the publication from 1976 of a succession of Australian dictionaries culminating in the definitive *Macquarie Dictionary* in 1981, and the triumphantly successful mounting of the 2000 Olympic Games in Sydney, to the formal declaration of the republic of Australia which is today but an ace away.

Yet what strikes a British eye and ear so forcibly 'down under' are the clear links to the United Kingdom and to Ireland. The Scottish name Macquarie pops up everywhere in

New South Wales – there's Macquarie Street and Macquarie University, half a dozen Macquarie Hotels and even a Macquarie Teashop. It's not surprising that the name has been memorialised because Scottish-born Major-General Lachlan Macquarie was one of the first great Australians, rising to become New South Wales's most famous Governor in 1809.

The connection with the Anglo-Saxon world is an inescapable fact of Australian history and, at every turn, signboards and social traditions proclaim it. The local café in Bathurst sells 'pies', 'pasties' and 'fish and chips'. The cars roll along the left-hand side of the wide streets past Bloom's 'chemist' shop and the local 'take-away', and fill up at the garage with 'petrol'. And in Bathurst's showground pavilions, they're serving tea and cakes and selling home-made 'sweets' (not 'candy') in a scene that could just as well be Newcastle-upon-Tyne as New South Wales.

Yet when you listen to the accents, savour the vocabulary, tune in to the distinctive tones of a nation at ease with its identity, it soon becomes clear that Australia possesses a language that is its own, that speaks for it and represents it with all the individuality that one would expect of an independent nation state.

That long road to individual identity began on board the vessel *Endeavour* just over 230 years ago. In 1768 Captain James Cook set sail from England to explore the territory of the southern Pacific Ocean. It was not by any means *terra incognita*. The Dutch had already made landfall in modern Tasmania and had named it Van Diemen's Land. The first Briton, the explorer and map-maker William Dampier, had landed in western Australia in 1688. And as **Frank Clarke**, Professor of Modern History at Sydney's Macquarie University, explained, he was not impressed.

On his third and last voyage in 1777, Captain James Cook landed at Adventure Bay, Van Diemen's Land (now Tasmania).

Dampier's original assessment was damning: 'The west coast of Australia is bleak, desert-like, inhospitable,' he said. He found the inhabitants to be the most primitive form of humanity he'd ever encountered. And that famous phrase about them having to keep their eyes almost closed to stop the flies from crawling in, which has bedevilled us ever since, was invented and publicised by Dampier.

In 1770, Cook and his crew were the first Europeans to set foot on the eastern seaboard. It was a moment of great solemnity and wonder, of discovery and novelty: one of those flash-of-lightning moments when names are bestowed, contrived, borrowed, misheard, and simply dreamed up from nothing. Think of the wonderment that Cook and his scientific officer Joseph Banks must have felt when confronted with the luxuriant and exotic foliage. Here were eucalypts in thickets, rich, glowing colours, parakeets shimmering through the undergrowth. **Frank Clarke:**

Cook wanted to call it 'Stingray Harbour' but changed the name in his journal to 'Botany Bay', I think in deference to Banks because of the number of interesting plant specimens he uncovered there, and to, I think, probably indicate in the nomenclature of the coastline that important scientific work was being done there. 'Stingray Harbour' was a bit descriptive – it's a bit like a sailor pulling something up that he can put on a plate. 'Botany Bay' has a different resonance altogether.

The shoreline, with its large expanses of grasslands and small clumps of trees, reminded Cook of a gentleman's park in England, but appearances were deceptive.

The Australian Aborigines

The Australian Aborigines are thought to have come originally from Asia and to have lived a nomadic existence as hunter-gatherers. When Cook arrived there were probably about 300,000 of them living in 250 tribal groups, each with their own territory, traditions, beliefs and language. There was no written language but customs and ideas were passed from one generation to the next through dance, storytelling and mythology. One of their most important beliefs centred on the idea of Dreamtime.

Dreamtime is the time when the natural environment was created and mythical beings with different powers walked the world. Some of them created humans. The idea is that Dreamtime goes on for ever and that the mythical beings still exist but they have changed into natural objects such as rocks or ponds. Human beings share a common life force with these mythical beings and with all nature. They must live together in harmony with each other and with nature, sharing their possessions and protecting their environment.

When the English settlers arrived the Aborigines thought they must be the spirits of their dead ancestors. At first they were friendly but later, as they observed the newcomers chopping down trees and destroying nature, they began to see them as enemies. In the ensuing conflict, thousands of Aborigines were killed, died of smallpox introduced by the settlers or were driven into the bush.

He and Banks assumed that this was the product of wild, untamed nature. We know now of course it was the product of regular fire-stick farming by Aborigines who had deliberately fired the land on a regular basis to keep it clear, to establish new grass growth for the support of the marsupials they favoured as food animals. So the landscape when Europeans arrived was a manufactured artefact, and they never knew it.

Today Botany Bay is a manufactured artefact right enough, and you hardly choose to go there for the wildlife. It is Sydney's vast container port, with jets roaring in over the cranes and oil storage tanks on their final approaches to Mascot international airport. The sandy shelving beach is attractive enough to a few scattered dog-walkers on a warm autumn afternoon, but the beach café is boarded up and the museum is closed most days of the week.

It is hard today to imagine the wilderness that the Englishmen set eyes on then. America had been colonised by Europeans for nearly 200 years and the English were well established in India when the crew of *Endeavour* encountered for the first time the Aboriginal inhabitants of this new continent. **Frank Clarke:**

Cook described the Aborigines as being 'in the liking of the noble savage of Rousseau', and so when the First Fleet [of convicts and military] **arrived** [eighteen years later] **they were predisposed to see noble savages. One of the officers, Arthur Fuller, was impressed by the bearing and the bravery of these people who tried to resist landings, standing on the beach waving spears and shouting defiance, and he described them as 'manly', and of course that name then was given to the district at the north head of the Sydney**

Harbour – it's one of our most beautiful beachside suburbs. And for some reason the other first settlers must have felt that was appropriate, because there are other occasions when [Governor] Phillip tries to label names on the countryside, and it just doesn't take. For example, the Blue Mountains [50 miles west of Sydney] **were named by Phillip as the 'Carmarthen Mountains', and quite simply nobody would use that. They looked blue, and they were the Blue Mountains, and that was all there was to it.**

On the southern shore of Sydney Harbour lies the heart of the city and the oldest part of the original settlement. Today the Circular Quay is the hub of Sydney's transport web, with skeins of ferry, bus and train lines spreading outwards across and along the harbour and the city. Look left from Circular Quay and you see the vast striding arc of the Harbour Bridge. Look right and there are the cream-coloured scooping sails of the still astonishing Opera House. It is the most wonderfully theatrical scene. Two hundred years ago the drama at the Circular Quay was a human one: 'THE CONVICT SHIP HAS ARRIVED!' is the headline on a contemporary newspaper advertisement. 'The Great Meeting will be held on the Circular Wharf To-day, at Noon, to Protest against the Landing of the Convicts. The Chair will be taken by Robert Lowe, Esq., the Member for the City. Let all places of business be closed! Let every man be at his post!'

Here, in the shadow of the tumble of Sydney's oldest buildings clinging to the slopes of The Rocks, moored the ships bringing their cargoes of men and women from Britain, and here still stands Cadman's Cottage, a humble harbourmaster's house built a couple of decades after the First Fleet arrived. It was here that I met **Susan Butler**, Publisher and Executive Editor of the most distinguished dictionary of Australian English, the *Macquarie Dictionary*.

Botany Bay, Sydney. The bay curves round into the south-eastern suburbs in the Randwick end of town, a straggle down the coast south of Bondi Beach.

We're standing at The Rocks, at the edge of Circular Quay, with the harbour shining behind us, and The Rocks in the early days were actually called 'The Gibbers', also because that was an Aboriginal Dharuk word, *gibber*, for 'stone' or 'rock'. And so the first contact between the convict colony and the Aboriginal community was with the speakers of the Dharuk language. The word 'gibber' in Australian English is actually now more limited to the sorts of rocks you find out in the outback: very hard, metallic sorts of rocks – we talk about 'gibber deserts' and things like that.

In fact the early days of the colony gave us a lot of borrowing from Aboriginal languages, particularly Dharuk, for animals and plants. The earliest instance of that is Captain Cook's boat, the *Endeavour*, which had sprung a leak off The Rocks and Cook had to land at the Endeavour River and fix up the boat. And he saw a kangaroo for the first time – he hadn't seen one earlier. So he asked the Aborigines there what it was called and they told him it was called a *kangaroo*. The word they used was somewhere between *kangaroo* and *gangaroo* which was then anglicised. And this is the pattern with a number of these Aboriginal borrowings that have a number of forms in their early life.

Despite the fact that, according to Frank Clarke, there were in the continent of Australia at least a quarter of a million Aborigines when the *Endeavour* reached Botany Bay, the effect on the language of the British who settled there was almost negligible. Melvyn Bragg spoke to **Dr Kate Burridge** of La Trobe University in Melbourne to find out just how much native Australian languages have marked the English of the continent.

It's estimated there would have been, around that time, roughly 200 different Aboriginal languages, but the influence was really very slight. Indeed I suppose you could compare it to the Celtic language influence on English in Britain – mainly place-names, flora and

fauna, cultural borrowings. There are plenty of place-names around Australia like Wagga Wagga, particularly with these reduplicated forms. Then there are cultural borrowings such as 'boomerang'. It's very typical that when you get newcomers coming into an area and the locals take up the language of those that come in, there's a period of bilingualism and then what you typically find is in fact very little influence in vocabulary.

A point reinforced by **Professor Frank Clarke**:

You can see certain words, like 'corroboree', or 'billabong' – the famous 'camped by a billabong' in *Waltzing Matilda* – those are Aboriginal words, and the call in the bush of 'cooee' is Aboriginal in origin. And if you look at the map of inland Australia you can see, in Western Australia for example, the Aboriginal Nunga dialect uses '-up' at the end of a word to indicate the presence of water. So if you look at the map you see Manjimup, Wallingup and Carinup and so on – they all indicate places with a water resource. In Sydney too you get Woolloomooloo and Ku-Ring-Gai – these are Aboriginal names.

Today the list of words in everyday Australian English that can be traced directly to one of the Aboriginal languages is relatively tiny. Yet most of them – 'boomerang', 'kangaroo', 'koala', 'kookaburra', 'corroboree' and so on – are terms that have become known as quintessentially Australian. The exception is in the far north of the continent where, as **Kate Burridge** observed, a rather different linguistic process took place.

Here you get pidgin Englishes that stabilised and turned into creole English; so in the north-west of Australia you find what are sometimes called 'creole continuums', so you get people speaking something called creole, which is not mutually intelligible to standard Australian English, and at the other end of the continuum speaking standard Australian English. And they have a range of all the varieties along that continuum.

'The KANGUROO an Animal found on the Coast of New Holland' – the kangaroo as first depicted by Cook's expedition to Australia in 1770.

Australian creole is strikingly different from standard English. When you see it written down it's tempting to think it's just a simplified sort of English, a sort of 'Me Tarzan, you Jane' view. But when you hear it spoken, in many aspects it's quite complex – much more complex than standard Australian. Take the pronoun system: Standard English has just one form 'we', so that if I said to you 'We're going now' you don't know whether you're included in that 'we' or who's exactly included in that 'we'. In creole they have four different 'we's. So there's a form for 'you-and-me' – the two of us, there's a form for 'me-and-somebody-else-excluding-you', there's a form for 'you-and-me-and-a-whole-heap-of-others', and there's a form for 'me-and-a-whole-heap-of-others-excluding-you'. So, much finer distinctions.

For the newly arrived Cook and Banks, the prospect of trying to communicate verbally with the Aboriginal peoples they encountered posed insurmountable problems. **Frank Clarke**:

The native languages in Australia were absolutely distinct and quite different from one another, unlike, say, in New Zealand where a Maori from anywhere in the two islands of New Zealand could speak to other Maoris. In Australia, once you took an Aborigine a short distance out of his traditional territory he was unable to communicate with other Aborigines any better than the Europeans could, and so you couldn't take a translator with you with any effectiveness.

Where Cook and his crew communicated with Aborigines at all it tended to be in terms of gifts, of body language. When the First Fleet arrives there's an account of Aborigines wanting to pull the trousers down of women and the men because they had never seen white men and they wanted to know what they were, whether they were human beings.

Once they'd established that the sailors had the proper equipment for a man, then everything was all right and they could understand what they were dealing with. So there were clearly some huge cultural barriers that had to be transcended on both sides, and language was just one of them.

The men and women who were convicted and sentenced to transportation to Australia provided a useful and profitable cargo for the ships plying the trade routes of the world. But according to **Frank Clarke**, the advantage was soon not only perceived to be with the shipowners. Within a few years, many former convicts – like John Cadman of Cadman's Cottage – found themselves doing well in the new colony.

To travel to Australia was to travel at government expense to a superior climate where you'd be better fed, better clothed and better housed than a free man or woman in Britain or a free man in the Army or the Navy. The discipline was fierce, but it was not as fierce as the armed services. Again you see the value of the convict to Australia: he's a source of labour. You flog a man so severely that he can't work – what's the point?

In the new penal settlement on the shores of the south Pacific, there were those who laboured and those who commanded. Inevitably, there was tension between them.

We see this for example in the first courts of the colony when Watkin Tench [Captain of Marines in the First Fleet] tells us in his diary that the British authorities needed a translator in the court in order to turn into middle-class English the dialects thick with thieves' slang that they were hearing from people in the dock; they couldn't understand what they were talking about. And so from the earliest days we have translators in the colonial courts to let the judges and the juries and the administrators know what the lower class are saying.

And with the translators came the first records of the particular linguistic usages commonly heard in Australia, as **Susan Butler** of the *Macquarie Dictionary* explained.

Our first Australian lexicographer was James Hardy Vaux. He was a convict – a forger, in fact, so he was a kind of middle-class, genteel convict if you like – but he certainly had a dictionary writer's instincts because he produced an account of the language of the settlements, of the convicts primarily, supposedly to explain their language to the judges. But what Vaux did in effect was give us an early record of words which became very important during the 1800s. A word like 'cove', for instance, was in fact thieves' slang, but it came to mean a person, in particular a person in some authority. So the man who ran the sheep or cattle station was referred to as the 'cove' or the 'boss'.

But not every term stayed around for very long:

For example, an expression like 'napping the Jacob from the danna drag'. 'Napping' is 'stealing', a 'Jacob' is a 'ladder' (as in 'Jacob's ladder'), and the 'danna drag' is the 'dunny can', the 'dunny cart' [sewage cart] – presumably dunny carts provided an easy source of ladders for people who wanted to rob buildings. So that was a sort of thieves' expression that died a death.

But other words, like 'gammon' for example, became important in Australian English. To 'gammon' someone was to fool them into thinking something, so it was a sort of con artist's trick. Nothing to do with ham, though. Its origin is unknown, but it certainly survived as an expression – 'Don't gammon me' you'd say to someone, if you're saying 'Come on, let's get real here, don't try and pull the wool over my eyes.'

Cadman's Cottage, Sydney, built in 1816.

Australia's convict past

Australia remained largely undeveloped for a long time after Captain Cook first laid claim to it. Although rich in natural resources it seemed too wild and impenetrable to be easily colonised and governed. To the British Government in the late eighteenth and early nineteenth century it simply seemed a good place to send people they wanted to get rid of. Instead of cluttering up the prisons, petty

As the new settlers reached for terms to interpret the new landscape they found themselves in, they quite understandably delved into the lexicon they brought with them. So birds and trees that reminded them of European varieties were named after them, regardless of any ornithological or botanical connection. Then there were those words which were also transplants but were applied differently – such as 'bush'. **David Blair**, Dean of Humanities at Macquarie University, gave an example.

Old words in new cultures always have to change. If you take a word like 'bush' for instance, which has quite a straightforward meaning in a British context, as soon as you move that word to an Australian environment, or indeed into a South African environment, it begins to look rather different. A bush at the bottom of the garden gets extended in Australia to mean territory which is covered by low trees, bushes or shrubs and ultimately to mean the countryside, or anything outside the major cities: we talk here about 'the city' or 'the bush'. Now that's clearly an extension of meaning which has never happened in Britain.

There was also a tendency for the settlers to seek familiarity – a sort of 'comfort blanket' – in the names they gave the places where they set up settlements. So in the Sydney area alone you can find yourself in Hyde Park, Kensington, Epping and Liverpool. **David Blair**:

You can go outside Sydney too and you can discover something about the settlement history. If you go north of Sydney to Newcastle you'll find a surprising number of place-names there which are very similar to those round Newcastle-upon-Tyne in Northumbria. The reason, of course, is that in Britain it was a coal-mining area and Newcastle here was a coal-mining area and it was settled by people from near Newcastle-upon-Tyne.

criminals and political dissidents were put on 'convict ships' and, after a long sea voyage in appalling conditions, unloaded to live out their sentences in the areas round the coast of Australia.

Most of the convicts were sent to work for the Government, often in chain gangs building roads or doing other public work. Some became 'assignees' – assigned to 'masters' for whom they worked until they had served their time. Then they were free to work for themselves – they became 'emancipists' and often lived respectable and prosperous lives.

Lachlan Macquarie, Governor of New South Wales from 1809 to 1821, soon recognised the important part that the emancipists could play in building the economy and the social framework of Australia. He appointed them as magistrates and public superintendents, and made it possible for them to have responsible jobs in the new industries and professions which were then getting started.

Coalminers came out here and brought the place-names with them. We even have a Wallsend up there – although no Hadrian's Wall I have to say!

Australian English has, since its inception, been characterised by the language of social division, of class. And today linguists divide up what is more or less a continuum of accent from the most marked to the least marked into three broad categories. In the 1960s two distinguished academics, Mitchell and Delbridge, were the first formally to identify and name these divisions. Working-class and rural Australian, typified by the character created by Paul Hogan in the *Crocodile Dundee* films, is the 'ocker' or Broad Australian speech. At the opposite end of the social spectrum Mitchell and Delbridge isolated that form of Australian which closely resembles British Received Pronunciation (RP), and which for many years – even while more earthy sounds were being heard in Britain – was adopted by the Australian Broadcasting Corporation as the 'gold standard' for their newsreaders. This was Cultivated Australian. And between the two extremes lay a vast (and, today, growing) middle ground which shared characteristics from both, which they referred to as General Australian.

Two hundred years ago, the seeds of such clear distinctions were being sown in the structure of the new colony's growing population of native-born Australians. Historian **Frank Clarke** of Sydney's Macquarie University explained that the social chasm extended to the vocabulary they used to describe themselves.

These were known as 'the currency'. They were called 'currency', as distinct from the English administrators who described themselves as 'pure sterling'. When the gentry in Australia had their native-born children they regarded themselves as 'pure merinos', whereas the others were mixed-race mongrels. So there was always this distinction, first

Australian English

In 1965 a book was published that celebrated spoken Australian and its 'ocker' pronunciation: *Let Stalk Strine*, by one Afferbeck Lauder ('alphabetical order'). It recorded such usages as 'gonnie?' ('do you have any?' as in 'Gonnie epples?'), 'harps' (thirty minutes past the hour, as in 'harps two'), and 'baked necks' (a popular breakfast dish, along with 'emma necks and 'scremblex'). Australian slang, too, is well documented – the Sydney Olympics website even included a short glossary for visitors of words such as 'bathers' or 'cossie' (swimsuit), 'thongs' (flip flops), 'pokies' (slot machines) and, of course 'Pom' (person from England).

Some slang words are enshrined in *Waltzing Matilda*. A 'swagman' is a drifter, carrying a 'swag' or pack as he goes looking for odd jobs. A 'squatter', surprisingly, was the wealthy landowner who might offer him work or shelter.

But today's slang is ever more colourful and varied. Someone who is stupid is a 'drongo' or a 'galah'. If they're lazy or don't pull their weight they're a 'no-hoper' or 'gutless wonder' who

of all between the British-born administrators and the British-born convicts, and then later on between the descendants of those two groups. There was always one with pretensions to be a gentry, an aristocracy, and the other group anxious to pull them down from their platforms and to level them. And that social tension is still to be found in Australia – it exists all the way through, this tension between the gentrified, educated side of the population and the lower orders.

Bruce Moore is editor of the *Oxford Australian Dictionary* and he explained how the names came about.

There was a shortage of sterling in the early days of the colony and all sorts of notes were used for exchange, and this came to be known as 'currency', so these were the sort of colonial notes as distinct from the sterling notes. People who were born in Australia thus came to be known as the 'currency lads and lasses' of the early colony, whereas people who were born and came across from Britain were described as 'sterling'. So that from the very early days of the colony, this quite significant tension develops into a linguistic clash, where the currency lads and lasses wore their Australianness and their language with a large amount of pride, and we get complaints from certain groups of society about people using colonial terms, supposedly new Australian terms, though in fact many of them originated in regional British usage.

The tensions between the first native-born Australians, defiantly proud of their new country, and the often authoritarian British ruling class have been part of the often tortured relationship between the two countries ever since. And, throughout, language has been there to interpret that relationship, between the linguistically approved and the linguistically oppressed. Lexicographer **Bruce Moore**:

'couldn't run guts for a slow butcher' or 'couldn't drag the skin off a rice pudding'. A 'chine' is a mate', a 'sort' is an attractive person, and someone flashy and vulgar is 'suave as a rat with a gold tooth'. If a man is particularly praiseworthy it's said that 'his blood's worth bottling'.

As in any language there are lots of words for money ('splosh', 'spondulicks', 'boodle') and for being drunk ('spiflicated', 'rotten', 'full as a boot'). If things are in disorder they are 'all over the place like a madwoman's breakfast'. If you lose your temper you 'spit the dummy' and the polite euphemism for farting is 'shooting a fairy'. If you don't believe what someone is telling you, you might say 'don't come the raw prawn with me' or 'come off the grass'. And if everything is going to be OK, 'she'll be apples'.

Some phrases such as 'buzz around like a blue-arsed fly' or 'better than a poke in the eye with a blunt stick' have become part of English usage, others remain part of an insider Australian language which changes almost as quickly as it can be enjoyed.

Our Prime Minister, Sir Robert Menzies, who retired in 1966, spoke a very correct English which we would now look back on and think of as being a very British form. Of course the general mob of punters out there spoke a very different kind of English, used all sorts of what were regarded as slang terms – we would now call them colloquialisms – and these, I think, were regarded as inferior and second-rate: even words such as 'dinkum' or 'fair dinkum', and 'cobber' meaning 'mate', that were certainly spoken throughout Australia. But they certainly didn't get – to use an Australian expression – didn't 'get a guernsey' [win approval] in any of the dictionaries that were being sold in Australia. So there was this odd sense that there were all these Australian terms, being used by Australians and which we regarded as being distinctively Australian, but which didn't find their way into the standard dictionaries. And that I think was therefore some kind of judgement that they were in fact substandard. And it's not until the 1970s that the language we speak finally found its way into our dictionaries.

'Dinkum', a word that we now associate exclusively with Australia, in fact originates in Britain, as **Susan Butler** of the *Macquarie Dictionary* pointed out.

'Dinkum' was a dialect word for work. In the novel *Robbery Under Arms* by the prolific nineteenth-century writer Rolf Boldrewood, there's a quote where the bush rangers are saying it took 'an hour's hard dinkum' to get to the top of the hill. And so 'fair dinkum' is 'a fair day's work for a fair day's pay' – a call for justice and reasonableness and fairness in dealing with people, which has been very strong in Australian English.

And it has needed to be. It's easy to forget both just how young and how vast the continent of Australia is. Fly north-west from Sydney and before long the terrain below turns to dusty reddish brown crisscrossed with dry watercourses. The inhospitable vastness of this huge continent stretches beneath for hundreds upon hundreds of miles, and it has taken many 'fair days' work' for the pioneering explorers, farmers and miners to tame it.

In Bathurst I was reminded of the 'fair dinkum' that sheep farmers had to turn in when I met Ray, who farms 3,000 merino sheep just outside the town. Ray, a 'bushie', had been hard at work 'crutching' his flock – shearing a small area of the fleece to stop soiling and subsequent infection. 'Stops the flies getting at them,' observed Ray's mate George, a smallholder. Complaints about the prices that wool was fetching dominated the talk: 'Cattle prices have never been better, lamb prices have never been better, so these blokes [cattle farmers] should all be smiling but they're still going crook.' 'Crook' is a classic Australian English term with a wide range of meanings, from 'sick' to – as in this case – 'whingeing' ('going crook').

I wondered about another term, 'dags'. 'That's what we crutch 'em for, to get rid of the dags,' said Ray. They turned out to be the clumps of wool hanging from the backsides of the sheep but, like 'crook', the meaning of the word can be far wider: 'You're a dag. He's a dag, this bloke,' added George's wife Val. **Dr Kate Burridge**, of La Trobe University in Melbourne, explained:

'Daggy' was a term for someone who was slovenly dressed, and then it back-formed to 'dag', who was also a bad dresser. And then it went through this curious shift to someone, oddly, who was very well dressed, and cool, and now in Australian English it's quite an affectionate term – someone who's 'a bit of a dag' is a bit of a clown.

But if the frontier spirit is still alive, it was in the nineteenth century that it was at its

peak. Then, the discovery of gold ore brought a huge charge of colloquialisms into Australian English. **Bruce Moore** edits the *Oxford Australian Dictionary*:

The terms arose in the 1850s and 1860s and, interestingly, they were published in the newspapers, which I think was important. Newspapers up until the 1850s were mainly reports of parliamentary proceedings here and in England. As soon as the gold rushes came along, most newspapers devoted in general about two pages of an eight-page newspaper to reports from the gold-fields which were written in the colloquial language of the gold-fields. And there was suddenly this huge tension in newspapers between the kind of language that was being used, say, on the first and second pages, which was very formal English, and this very different kind of language, the language that people really spoke on the gold-fields.

So **Bruce Moore** identifies 'to fossick' – meaning 'to find gold' – as a gold-field term that gained currency and then became transferred to more general usage. More unfamiliar was 'mullock':

'Mullock' was mining refuse in the 1850s, 1860s: you would have 'a load of mullock' over there – a load of rubbish. And that's now a standard term – people say 'What the politicians are telling us is just a load of mullock.'

In Bruce Moore's *Oxford Australian Dictionary* there are literally thousands of terms which are credited as being of Australian origin, including such striking local usages as 'abso-bloody-lutely'.

Now some people would simply regard this as sort of inferior slang, but we regard this as an important feature of Australian English. In any Australian dictionary that we produce

we want to show how Australian English is used, so that a word such as that certainly has to be included.

So along with the characteristic accent the other striking feature of the language is the slang. This, understandably, is found particularly in spoken Australian, though it also makes its way into poetry and novels. But I was struck by an instance where popular Australian usage was firmly enshrined in print – a poster for the Salvation Army proclaiming 'The Salvos never give up caring'. **Dr Kate Burridge**:

I think if you asked me what was the most distinctive feature of Australian English, aside from the accent, it would be the love of abbreviations, but not just simply abbreviating but tacking on an ending – either the '-o' ending or the '-ie' ending. So you get things like 'Robbo, the weirdo journo from Freeo ended up on dero and metho'; or 'I took some speccie piccies of us opening our Chrissie pressies at brekkie' – I mean, that's an exaggeration. These endings are found in other varieties of English but here they have quite different meanings I think. People wrongly call them diminutives, which are 'fondling' endings that you put on something that you have a warm affectionate feeling towards – I'm sometimes called 'Kato', for instance. But when you get it on someone who works on the wharf who is a 'wharfie', or a musician is a 'muso', there's something else going on there. I don't call a politician a 'pollie' because I think of the politician as a warm, endearing creature!

And there is nothing particularly endearing either about what is perhaps the best known '-o' form of Australian, 'arvo', for 'afternoon'. A socio-linguist has claimed that this feature is 'a linguistic enactment of the Anglo-Australian self-image', with its cult of informality and egalitarianism – as **Kate Burridge** put it, 'a sort of casual, laid-back toughness and good humour, with a hefty dollop of anti-intellectualism thrown in'.

There is an association in Australian English speakers' minds between short words and friendliness, so you'd get great hulking Australian blokes talking about 'mozzie' for a 'mosquito' or a 'maggie' for a 'magpie', but you wouldn't get them saying 'birdie' or 'doggie' – so-called diminutive endings, or nursery talk.

But what determines whether a word should take '-ie' or '-o' is unclear:

I mean why is a musician called a 'muso' and not a 'musie' and why is a 'wharfie' called a 'wharfie' and not a 'wharfo'? These endings deserve more scholarly attention than they're typically given I think.

Back in Bathurst, such academic linguistic niceties seem, well, academic. The Centenary of Federation celebrations are drawing to an end and the Golden Kangaroos Marching Band have made their way to the old Courthouse, along with the floats, Cobb and Co's stagecoach and the historical re-enactment society. The streets are swathed in banners, the queues of cars are held by the police cordon to let the parade pass. The pride in being Australian, in speaking Australian, is everywhere evident. It is not a raucous, tub-thumping, corrosive nationalism. This is a quiet and, above all, confident sense of identity – British maybe in heritage, linguistically too, but today uncompromisingly Australian, with values and traditions that are uniquely Australian and a language that echoes, reflects and enshrines them.

5

South African English

A Trek to Freedom

Previous page: Soweto, Johannesburg, June 1976. Over 100 were killed during protests against the use of Afrikaans in schools.

Right: Nelson Mandela on the day of his release from imprisonment on Robben Island, 11 February 1990.

Far right: A photograph showing political prisoners being released, part of a poster on Robben Island.

Of the many memorable images on television over the past twenty years, few have had greater power to delight and move in equal measure than that of the stately walk to freedom of Nelson Mandela. The date was 11 February 1990. Mandela, subsequently the first black President of South Africa, has become one of the iconic figures of our time, but for years the country he came to rule over provoked worldwide political, cultural and social isolation and opprobrium during the white-supremacist era of apartheid.

There can be few territories in the world which embrace English as a principal language where the way you speak says quite so much about your political and cultural values. Language is a badge here unlike almost anywhere else. Mandela's speech is a stately, gentle English that beneath its measure and moderation holds the power and iron will of determination and the strength that carried him through his long years of imprisonment on Robben Island. Mandela's English has equally become the sound of the new South Africa.

Apartheid spoke with the language and accents of the Afrikaner minority. In South Africa, the freedom struggle and the enfranchisement of the 70 per cent African population were represented – amongst the multiplicity of indigenous languages – above all by English. Afrikaans and those who spoke it were associated with the whites-only policy, social exclusion and injustice. Afrikaner ways and the Afrikaans language will, it seems to me, be for many years stigmatised, and at least in the eyes of the rest of the world will bear the stamp of the loathsome discriminatory regime that used it.

Although always a minority language – spoken by about 3.6 million people out of a total population of more than 40 million – today it is English that holds linguistic pole-

position in South Africa. **Penny Silva** is Director of the *Oxford English Dictionary*, Editor of the *Oxford Dictionary of South African English* and herself a South African from the Eastern Cape. The new-found strength and influence that English is enjoying in post-apartheid South Africa, she says, has not been met with unalloyed joy.

English has a very powerful role in South Africa today. It's quite a paradoxical role, I feel. People have a mixed attitude to it if it's not their own language. It's seen as a major resource, and for the upwardly mobile it's the language of business, education, the media, international discussion. And so people have a tremendous ambition to learn it and to speak it well. But I would say that it's also seen as probably a bit of a juggernaut, and I think there's a lot of worry amongst speakers of the smaller languages in South Africa, especially the African languages, that English is going to sweep all before it. But there's no doubt that it has played an extremely important role in communication, starting really from the time of the negotiations, just before the change of government. For quite a few decades it had been a Cinderella, and I think at that point it came back into its own again.

With Nelson Mandela's ascent to power, the Afrikaans-speaking and Afrikaans-influenced English-speaking minority were marginalised. That is not to say that all words of Afrikaans origin bear this stigma, though clearly 'apartheid' itself and 'laager' (originally encampment) have associations that will mark them for ever, even when taken outside the strictly African arena. Thus an expression like 'cultural and social apartheid' takes the word well beyond its original South African meaning of 'separate development', picking up the pejorative tenor of the regime's associations in the wider world. Likewise, the instruments of apartheid – the hated Pass Laws, and 'homelands', the name given by whites to the 'African' areas of the country – belong to a vocabulary whose role is today largely historical.

But you do not have to look very hard in day-to-day British and American English to find unstigmatised Afrikaans words. In fact, you need look no further than volume one of encyclopaedias which kick off with 'A to aardvark'. At the other end of the shelf, as it were, you find 'veld' and 'Voortrekker'. Along the way, the linguistic 'spoor' indicates traces of the pioneering spirit that characterised the South African experience, the great 'trek', and wildlife such as the 'wildebeest' and the 'springbok'.

If English with an African – rather than a strictly South African – accent is the new way in the land, the language has a long history there, although the colonisation of South Africa by the British took place a little later than that of Australia, for example. The first European settlers in South Africa were the Dutch, in a colony founded in 1652 at Cape Town in the shadow of Table Mountain by a merchant of the Dutch East India Company, Jan van Riebeeck. Many shiploads of settlers and refugees landed at the Cape over the next hundred years, but in 1795, during the Napoleonic Wars and amid tension between the administration and the citizens, a British expeditionary force arrived, drove out the Dutch and annexed the colony for the Crown with the subsequent establishment of British control eleven years later.

The Eastern Cape was the site of the first major British settlement, where 5,000 men and women were granted land. English was the natural language that they brought to their new country, and by 1822, it was established as the official language of the Cape, used for all legal, administrative and educational purposes. **Penny Silva** described these speakers of Eastern Cape English.

They were a remarkably mixed group of people, from gentlemen with their carriages and their servants right the way down to labourers and shoemakers from inner London, from Scotland, Ireland – from across the whole of the United Kingdom. It was a government-sponsored immigration and it was post Napoleonic Wars, and I think in a way it was a useful way of getting the disaffected out of Britain. But it was also seen as a bit of an adventure by some more wealthy people. So you had a range of regional and educational dialects and standards of English which was an extremely mixed bunch.

They travelled in 'parties' as they were called, which were generally sponsored by somebody who was well-off. Quite small groups settled in these 'parties' in various areas around Grahamstown in Eastern Cape and of course being a small area meant that you rubbed shoulders with people. It's been claimed that, despite the various dialects and educational forms of English that you got by the time the children of that generation had grown up, one regional South African English had developed.

Meanwhile, 10,000 Dutch farming settlers, discontented with the protection the British authorities were affording them, began in 1835 to fan out northwards and eastwards in the Great Trek (the *Groot Trek*), gathering in what would become the Orange Free State and later in Natal. Battles with the indigenous Zulus weakened the so-called Voortrekkers and by 1842 the British had annexed their Port Natal (today's Durban). Thousands of British settlers now sailed for these newly acquired territories and the discovery of gold and diamond-bearing rocks brought, in the 1870s, the customary rush of immigrants from Europe in search of personal enrichment. From

To give a flavour of the language that the British settlers of South Africa found themselves confronting, here is the Twenty-Third Psalm in Afrikaans:

Die Here is my herder, ek kom niks kort nie.
Hy laat my in groen weivelde rus.
Hy bring my by waters waar daar vrede is.
Hy gee my nuwe krag.
Hy lei my op die regte paaie
tot die eer van sy Naam.
Selfs al gaan ek deur donker dieptes,
sal ek nie bang wees nie, want U is by my.
In U hande is ek veilig.

U laat my by 'n feesmaal aansit,
terwyl my teestanders moet toekyk.
U ontvang my soos 'n eregas,
ek word oorlaai met hartlikheid.
U goedheid en liefde
sal my lewe lank by my bly
en ek sal tuis wees
in die huis van die Here
tot in die lengte van dae.

then to the end of the Victorian era, close on half a million newcomers, many with English as their mother tongue, began a new life in southern Africa.

With such a chequered and densely woven history of settlement, conflict, expeditionary enterprise and greed, it is little surprise to learn that, in the words of the world's leading chronicler of the English language today, Professor David Crystal, 'the English language history of the region thus has many strands'. Mother tongue to Londoners who settled the Cape and Midlanders who went to Natal, English was also the second language of the Dutch settlers, the Boers.

The most widely spoken non-African language of South Africa is Afrikaans. Today it is regarded as a separate entity rather than as a dialect or variant of Dutch, though it only took shape as a formal language towards the end of the nineteenth century. During the early days of Dutch settlement it was known variously as Cape Dutch or South African Dutch, or simply 'the *taal*' (language) of hearth and home, and it was used alongside the formal speech of the Netherlands. Now, 8 million South Africans are reckoned to speak Afrikaans, with a further million and a half in Namibia. In today's democratic South Africa, it is one of the eleven official languages, alongside English, Ndebele, Pedi, Sotho, Swazi, Tsonga, Tswana, Venda, Xhosa and Zulu.

Afrikaans speakers are by no means exclusively white, yet in recent history the language has been deeply mired in the racist administrations of the apartheid era. In fact, despite the centuries of linguistic interaction between the communities there are still, it seems, strong divisions in South Africa between those who speak English and those who retain Afrikaans as their first language of choice. I was surprised to see the following disclaimer on an internet site devoted to the language which apologised to its

In the classical English version of the King James Bible:

The Lord is my shepherd; I shall not want.
He maketh me to lie down in green pastures:
He leadeth me beside the still waters.
He restoreth my soul:
He leadeth me in the paths of righteousness
For his name's sake.
Yea, though I walk through the valley of the
shadow of death,
I will fear no evil: for thou art with me;

Thy rod and thy staff they comfort me.
Thou preparest a table before me
In the presence of mine enemies:
Thou anointest my head with oil;
My cup runneth over.
Surely goodness and mercy
Shall follow me all the days of my life:
And I will dwell in the house of the Lord
For ever.

readers: 'In this project you might find some weird and terrible spelling and grammatical mistakes. This is probably due to none of the team members speaking English as a first language, but as a second.'

The influence of Afrikaans on South African English should not be underestimated. About half the words in the national lexicon that are distinctively South African originate in Afrikaans: words such as 'kloof' (valley), 'veld' (open country) and 'dorp' (village). Melvyn Bragg asked **Penny Silva** when this process of assimilation began.

They started from the very first day. People landed on the beach at Port Elizabeth and they were collected by Dutch farmers in their wagons and taken up the country to the area of Grahamstown, and they picked up words. You could imagine somebody sitting in the back of a wagon and pointing at an animal or a plant that they saw and the Dutch farmer giving them the name of it.

In the early diaries, in the first few months, you find the words just popping up as though they're known already. They arrived in April 1820 and by late April, early May, the diaries are starting to reflect words like 'kraal' as the word for a cattle enclosure, and like 'Boer', because of the farmers' names for themselves. You get a lot of wagon terminology too – 'trek' for the journey that you do, the 'voorloper' for the man who led the cattle. The 'voorloper' was a young boy usually who took the 'riem' as it was called – the leather thong – and led the oxen along. And your wagon pole, to which the oxen were attached was called the 'disselboom', and that starts coming in with all sorts of odd, strange spellings. 'Thistleboon' was one Anglicised form of it. The wagon chest was the 'voorkis', and that replaces English in most of the diaries that you find – all sorts of quite technical language coming in from the whole business of using wagons and travelling.

The springbok was first used as an emblem in 1906 by the national rugby team, and was later adopted by other sports. However, the national teams were for whites only and with the end of apartheid there was strong pressure to remove the springbok. The cricket team replaced it on their badge with the national flower, the protea. The rugby team was against changing their emblem, but the problem was resolved in their favour at the start of the 1995 Rugby World Cup, held in South Africa, when President Mandela appeared in the team's green and gold jersey, complete with springbok emblem, and urged everyone in the country, black and white, to support 'our boys'.

One can imagine some of those early, rather grand settlers insisting on as English a diet as possible. But new climates demand new ways and food inevitably became another area where the influence of the Cape Dutch speakers came to bear.

You had your food that you ate on the trek. One was dried meat, which was called 'biltong' – and that's a staple food in South Africa today. Because it didn't rot of course it was stored on the wagon. And you had hardened rusks called 'beskuit' which people chewed as they went along. When you started, you 'inspanned' and when you stopped you 'outspanned', and those were Anglicised versions of the Afrikaans words. So I think their whole vocabulary was integral to the actions that they were following.

And in fact nineteenth-century writers talk about this in quite glowing terms, wondering how people would exist without all these words in this country: 'We need all of these words,' they say. 'We don't have "glens" and "cliffs" any more, we have "kloofs" and "kranses"' – which are Dutch words again. So the language does reflect the whole geography and the activities that are different from what people were used to.

If the Cape Dutch speakers contributed the largest number of items to the South African lexicon, at 10 per cent the influence of indigenous African languages is also considerable. The most important is that of the Khoi, a collective term for a large number of gentle, pastoral small tribes of indigenous African people (who were not Bantu), found all along the Cape coast from Cape Town into the interior. They were previously known by the term – now deemed unacceptable – Hottentot. The Khoi contributed the click sounds to the Xhosa language, and to English such words as 'gnu'. **Penny Silva**:

A very central word in South African English from the Khoi language is the local word for 'ouch', which in South African English is 'eina'. I don't think any South African children would say 'ouch!', they all say 'eina!', so it is interesting how some of the most well-used and central vocabulary items are borrowed from the languages that the settlers met up with in the 1820s.

One of the huge changes in post-apartheid South Africa has been the re-empowerment of the African majority, for whom the English language represented a pathway and a voice for freedom, for solidarity with other black peoples, a voice that could be heard throughout the world. The great South African actor **John Kani** was born in Port Elizabeth, where those first settlers landed in 1820, and he feels deeply the connection with the English language they disembarked with – as well as with his indigenous Africanness. But he is also conscious of the ambiguities that using the language of the colonial master represents.

It was Sir Rufane Donkin, then Governor of the Cape Province, who, when his wife Elizabeth died, named my town in memory of her. That's why we are called Port Elizabeth. Actually the right name for my town is Cacadu, but this is one of the things that now we are correcting as a new government in the democracy.

The first thing the English did was to 'educate the native', immediately missionary work and also school work. So we became, in Port Elizabeth, an English city. I still remember as a young boy that there were even debating societies. Affluence and learnedness was judged by how you spoke English. We even spoke about 'the Queen's language'. When I in the fifties started going to school my father used to boast that they used to do the 'Royal Readers' – they were old literature that used to be shipped from England. But they

John Kani, actor, writer and Artistic Director of
the Market Theatre of Johannesburg.

were very proud of use of the English language. My father was proud that we were colonised by the British instead of the Germans or the Belgians or the French, who come in and eradicate the existing natives' culture and impose their own culture on it. At least the British he felt were trying to make us very sophisticated and learned gentlemen! It was a pure instrument of subjugating our people. So the learning of English made you a better servant. You were then at least accessible to the master.

But Kani's generation saw the relationship with English somewhat differently. With independence from Britain granted in 1931 and accepted by South Africa in 1934, a policy of segregation and the creation of 'homelands' for the black population began. When the largely Afrikaner National Party won the parliamentary election of May 1948, the primacy of the English language was challenged by the dominant Afrikaans-speaking whites. For **John Kani** and his fellow English-speaking black South Africans, their language now symbolised more than a tool of Empire.

We turned it around as the most powerful weapon of making the master understand in his language, understand in his culture, that we are free Africans and this is our land. The thing that promoted English was that the Africans immediately recognised Afrikaans as the language of the oppressor, so they then preferred basically to speak English, because after 1948 it's almost as if the English began to say 'It's not us, it's them! As far as we are concerned you could be free today – though we will do nothing about it, we will not assist you in getting free today – but do not blame us any more. We're not in government, we're now in opposition.'

Penny Silva, of the *Oxford Dictionary of South African English*, detailed the role of English as the voice of opposition in the country.

English was the language of the struggle and the ANC adopted it as its language and therefore it had a very different feel to it. It was also the language of access to the international media, and it was the language that people used when they were exiles very often. And particularly in the seventies when Afrikaans was attempting to move into schools as a language of education. For instance, in Soweto the 1976 riots were sparked off because there was an attempt to teach mathematics and a couple of other subjects in Afrikaans.

English maintained its neutrality, although I think some academics would deny that it was a neutral language – it has its own colonial baggage – but it's probably the most neutral there can be in South Africa at the moment. Afrikaans has a history which is not acceptable as a national language, and as for the African languages, it would be very difficult to choose one because there'd be a huge emotional reaction, I think. So English can be seen as a useful neutral lingua franca.

Judge Albie Sachs, a lawyer and a prominent member of the African National Congress who worked tirelessly for independence and who was badly injured in a car bomb attack in 1988, offered his view of the way English grew to be the mouthpiece of the struggle. For Sachs, it was not so much a deliberate policy.

It never happened formally, there was never a decision like that – in practice people could speak in Zulu, Xhosa, Afrikaans, and frequently did at meetings. But it was just so damn convenient often to use English, to have minutes in English. And yet the songs were in different languages – a lot of the emotion, a lot of the chatting would be quite spontaneously done in the different languages. It wasn't a formal, official decision that was taken. But it did become very much the language of debate, the language of most publications.

As so often in our visual age, it was the signs that were the most visible manifestation of apartheid. And though they were only the visual tip of a very real and vicious horror, **John Kani** remembers just how hurtful they could be to a young child, as 'all the luxuries of my town' – the parks he played in – suddenly, following the 1948 election, sprouted *Net Blankes* signs: 'For Whites Only'. Sometimes, too, the segregation would be linguistically hidden.

Near our terminus there was a beautiful sign which said 'Public toilets'. It simply means 'everybody can use them'. But in my language, Xhosa, it says 'Toilets for non-whites only'. But for the tourists who don't speak Xhosa, it says 'Public toilets'. And it would mean they began to hide petty apartheid very well.

John Kani, after demeaning jobs at a car factory, eventually got a job as a mechanic, though his wage was strictly controlled by the laws that forbade Africans from earning the same wage as whites for the same job. He used his experiences in his budding career on the stage. Should, though, the medium of expression be Xhosa, with its limited scope for understanding across South Africa's linguistically diverse culture, or was English, as lingua franca, the most effective means to express the Africans' plight?

English became the bridging language that would make communication easier and facilitate the spreading of the message through all the peoples of the land. We were aware that we were using English for this purpose, though in the process of making the work we would use the first-language 'feel'.

At the same time an English arose which was like the way we speak in South Africa, which combines some word – like I would say 'We must have an *indaba* quickly', meaning 'We

must have a quick meeting.' The word *indaba* in Xhosa means a meeting. Or we may use for instance an Afrikaans word, that there was a *bosberaad* – it simply means there was a political meeting, somewhere. So we began to integrate in the English as in the spoken language some of the words that come from our own language, and that developed, though not to the extent of the West Indies where a patois language emerged.

So English could be an instrument of understanding, communication and self-expression. Yet **John Kani** told a story that encapsulates the ambiguous feelings that many black South Africans must feel towards the language. It went back to his schooldays and the regime of Dr Verwoerd, later to be assassinated.

I still remember our teacher reading this policy document which was smuggled out of Parliament, in which Dr Verwoerd was warning the Cabinet that '… in educating the African, one: do not make a mistake of creating another Englishman who will grow and be opposition to us. Two: in educating the African do not mislead him into thinking that upon the attainment of certain educational qualifications that the country's racial policies will disappear. Three: educate the African within his place of employment, never beyond or above.' There was the use of English, to hurt me. There was the use of English by the master, by the racist government. He knew I would understand it in English, so he wrote it in English, and that made me hate English, because it was the oppressive language in its form.

But for the ANC lawyer **Albie Sachs**, English managed to transcend its associations and, in the words of Nigerian writer Wole Soyinka, 'twist the linguistic blade in the hands of the traditional cultural castrator and [carve] new concepts into the flesh of white supremacy'.

We grasped English, our people took over English, wrote marvellous books and stories and poems and songs in English, it became our English, it became part of our language, indigenised in many ways. We fought for freedom using the English language.

Oppression, justification for oppression, terrible laws, hanging, whipping, prisons, dispossession, taxation, were all done in the English language, but at the same time resistance was also in English. And it became a very convenient medium to enable people speaking different African languages and Afrikaans to communicate with each other in a common cause without suppressing the other languages. I think that's the way in which English now becomes one of our languages, a very convenient language, the main second language in South Africa, but not hegemonic language.

So far we have seen how English interacted with Cape Dutch and Afrikaans, to an extent too with Xhosa – and the other official languages have similar levels of mixing. But one of the major strands in the social and linguistic structure is the large population of South Africans of Indian origin who arrived there around 1860. **Raj Mesthrie**, Professor of Linguistics at the University of Cape Town, is himself of Indian origin and he explained the history of the complex relationship between the cultures.

From 1860 onwards, ship after ship brought Indians in their hundreds of thousands to Natal to labour, to set up plantations – these were mainly sugar cane plantations – and to labour in them. And it's a diverse community speaking at least five or six languages even today including Hindi, Tamil, Telagu, Gujarati, Urdu, and finally in Cape Town a small language called Kokani which originated south of Bombay.

With diverse backgrounds and languages from all over India, these Indian workers needed a 'bridging language' between themselves and they used a pidginised form of

An apartheid notice in English and Afrikaans on a beach near Cape Town, denoting the area for whites only.

Zulu – the majority African language – called Fanagalo. But, as remarked on by Mahatma Gandhi when he lived there, the South African Indian community also used a very widespread form of 'broken English'. With the advent of apartheid in 1948, the Indians found themselves segregated from other races, black and white.

You went to a school for Indians taught by Indian teachers and school principals, you went to your university, as I did in the late 1970s, to an Indian university. So there was a tremendous inbreeding, an inculcation, a reinforcement of this somewhat broken English. It had already had its roots prior to 1948, but for the long years between 1948 and the end of apartheid in 1990, people really made this variety into their own.

In this dialect, things that might strike others as being ungrammatical have stabilised and are used by educated and uneducated people. For example, in standard British English you have what we call a 'tag', so you'll say 'John came, didn't he?' The 'didn't he?' is a tag. Or you would say 'Jill is your sister, isn't she?', so we always add a verb and a pronoun at the end as a kind of tag. Now in many varieties of English throughout the world the rules are too complex because you have a choice of pronouns, you have a choice of verbs – you could say 'isn't', 'aren't', 'weren't', 'didn't', 'don't'. And in many varieties of English one universal tag is used, and in India it is 'isn't it?'. So you would say 'Jill is your sister, isn't it?', or 'You are coming, isn't it?' In South Africa this has stabilised, and we've reduced it even further to simply 'isn't?'. So you would say 'Joan is coming, isn't?', and that means 'Joan is coming, isn't she?'. Or 'He did it, isn't?', and that means 'He did it, didn't he?'

The story of English in South Africa is as complex and as layered as the 350-year history of the territory since those first Dutch settlers built their stockade under Table

Mountain. We can but scratch the surface, therefore, but we should perhaps conclude with one story of what has happened since democracy arrived. It is a story of a linguistic purge. Words have been stigmatised and the stigma removed under different regimes and cultural systems since time – and language – began. But even the prescriptive and proscriptive Académie Française has not gone to quite the lengths seen in South Africa. Here certain terms are not only discouraged but actually banned. The most offensive term, widely used during the apartheid era, was the derogatory 'kaffir'. **Penny Silva** of the *Oxford Dictionary of South African English*:

It is actually from Arabic and it means 'infidel'. It was used down the east coast of Africa, but it's like 'nigger', it's as appalling, and it was used in everyday speech all the time by, for instance, policemen arresting people on the Pass Laws, people being put into jail for hardly anything. If a white person was walking down the street and a black person got in their way they would be told 'Kaffir, get out of my way!' It was that kind of appalling racial contempt which really hit at the core of people's beings. And it was so strongly regarded that it is now in fact illegal to use it, and if you use it you can be taken to court and you can be charged with what's called 'crime and injury', which is derogatory behaviour, insult.

But the word 'kaffir' goes back, it's almost one of the oldest words there is in South African English in that it's noted as the word for black people in the subcontinent by the earliest travellers – late 1500s, early 1600s. And it's had a very chequered history in that it was a purely descriptive term in the beginning: it wasn't seen as an insult at all. And it was really only at the beginning of the twentieth century that it took on its contemptuous nature, I would say. But because of that apartheid stigma that it held, there was a very strong reaction against it being included in our dictionary.

Which it is. Because even in the tortured history of the nation of South Africa, dictionaries must hold all words, abusive, reviled and dangerous, as well as heart-warming, empowering and liberating. Such is the endless variety and richness of language. Actor **John Kani**:

The English language is able to evoke within the culture of people that catalyst that made them go back to their language with greater pride and greater interest of finding out more about it. Because it could even be explained in English how important it is not to lose your language, how important it is to hold on to your culture, how important it is to retain the Xhosa in you – all this could be explained in English. So the English became a used tool for us, to further our own aims of the African agenda.

When I stand on the stage as Othello, don't be misled, I'm thinking in Xhosa, I'm not thinking in English. I still go to sleep at night and dream in my native language. I have to dream in Xhosa. But my children grow up with the two languages at the same time from age one day. We speak to them all in both languages – I have eight children – so they are quite conversant with both languages. So we're able to cross-think in both languages.

So we have colonised English to make it serve us in repayment of what Queen Victoria did to us. So we have a slave called English, and it serves us well.

6

English
Without Roots

Have you ever been confronted with an expression or a word in a book or newspaper that you feel you should understand, yet cannot actually explain? Do you go back and read it again to see if you have missed a vital clue? Or maybe you move on to the next sentence in the hope of finding enlightenment there. One such example that had me perplexed for weeks was the phrase 'to take a rain check'. Suddenly, it seemed, everyone on radio and television and in the newspapers was hard at it taking these confounded rain checks. I did the reading forward and backward trick, and it seemed quite clear from the context that the phrase meant 'to defer the pleasure' or 'to decline an offer' that had been proposed; bluntly, 'to say no'. But what was with the rain, and why did it need checking? A few discreet enquiries eventually gave me the answer. It is an American expression, drawn from the world of outdoor events such as baseball, where ticketholders who turn up only to have the game rained off are entitled to a free voucher for another day. Simple, really, when you understand the context.

But then, as the phrase goes, context is all. Imagine an American picking up a British newspaper and reading that a politician 'hit his opposite number for six'. Or indeed 'bowled him a googly'. Images drawn from sport pepper everyday conversation, and while some ('three strikes and you're out') have sufficient internal logic to carry them beyond their local context (baseball in this case), many come directly from the shared experiences of one nation or group of nations. No problem, then with six-hitting in the Commonwealth where the sun has always shone on cricket – a positive advantage, indeed, in countries like India, Pakistan, Sri Lanka and Australia where cricket has the status of national obsession. But in the American zone, no dice.

It is this local cultural context that comes into play when people speak of the

globalisation of English. We have seen how the English language has taken its different paths across the planet, mutating along the way and, at its various destinations, developing a local character with distinctive accent, lexicon and slang. **David Graddol** is a lecturer at the Open University and has studied and written extensively about the way English has gradually assumed this world role. He believes that users of the different Englishes will need to find ways to understand one another.

I think anything which is strongly marked as a British variety of English will be seen increasingly as some kind of regional or local identity marker. And I will have to think, for example, as I go around the world and use English, 'Do I want to sound quite so British, or do I want to converge in some way perhaps with the English used by most of my audience?' And that may be done in simple ways by pronouncing 'r's more, by changing the words that I'm using, and it will represent a shift of identity, a flattening of my British identity for an international audience. I see that as inevitable.

Of course, it is not so difficult to adapt one's pronunciation or avoid using expressions that will be incomprehensible to people whose cultural context is different. The critical question is how much cultural 'flavour' can one preserve without mystifying? How much meaning, too, is bound up with that flavour? We noted earlier that when Americans use 'city' to describe any community, regardless of size or the possession of a cathedral, the flavour or 'cityness' of the word is completely lost.

Humour, too, like imagery, often needs to be securely nested within national cultural references in order to work effectively. Esperanto, the language invented in the last years of the nineteenth century by the Polish linguist Zamenhof, has no such cultural context, and I once asked an eminent British Esperantist whether it could be used to pun and crack jokes in. 'Of course,' he said, surprised by my lack of faith. But can a language like English, when shorn of all or most of its cultural flavour, have any value?

Observing ardent Esperantists travelling the world, discoursing freely with Chinese, Japanese, Poles and Hungarians at their regular international congresses, makes one realise that the goal of mutual comprehensibility is a rare prize indeed. Esperanto is widely spoken, broadcast in and used for every sort of cultural manifestation (Gilbert and Sullivan in Esperanto? – no problem), but, sadly for Dr Zamenhof and his enthusiasts, it has never really been a serious option as a world language.

Today, it is English that claims the prize. And why? The answer is simple, and it helps to explain why Esperanto has never really made serious headway as a world language – power. **Professor David Crystal** is Britain's foremost academic expert and writer on the English language, and his book *English as a Global Language* offers a thorough guide to the relentless rise of the language across the world.

Power is the key here. But there are many kinds of power – four kinds of power I think. There's the power that goes with the British Empire – political, military might – and that was the first sort of power that pushed English on its way. But that didn't last forever as we now know. Secondly, following on from that in the eighteenth century, there was the power of technology – scientific power, the Industrial Revolution. Something like half the people who made that revolution possible – the macadam and the steam engines and the textile mills – worked in the medium of English, either in Britain or in America. And then, in the nineteenth century, the third kind of power, economic power – power where 'money talks', and the money that was talking was the dollar very largely. At the beginning of the nineteenth century the number one productive nation was Britain. By the end of the

nineteenth century it was America. Either way it was an English-speaking country and economic power pushed English forward then. And fourthly, in the twentieth century, cultural power, in the sense that every significant cultural development in the twentieth century either started in an English-speaking country or was facilitated very rapidly by an English-speaking country – for example cinema, which crucially became developed through Hollywood.

It is curious that this complicated tongue of ours with its irregularities and its infernally unphonetic written forms (think of 'though', 'thought', 'through' and 'tough') should now be generally accepted as the lingua franca of the world. Not only can the British, Americans, Australians, many Indians, Africans and others who have English as their first language make themselves freely understood to each other, but a Chinese businessman can talk to his Czech customer in English, the Belgian president of the International Olympic Committee can express his goals for the movement to the world's press in English, and even the French, for whom *le français* has always been a matter of national pride, are frequently now heard voicing their official comments in the international arena in English. Interestingly, **David Graddol** claims the global status of English to be a phenomenon with a much longer pedigree than is generally assumed.

I think we now have a tendency of thinking of the spread or rise of global English as a late twentieth-century phenomenon. What I find very interesting is the way people were talking at the end of the nineteenth century in a very very similar way. People were talking about how English was going to be the language of the future, about how it was going to be driven around the world by world trade and by technology.

This was actually a phenomenon particularly in Europe – Germans, Swiss, people both in the business world and in the world of language, talking up English and trying to estimate how many millions or even billions of speakers there would be within about a century. A case in point in about 1872 was when the first Japanese envoy to Washington made a presentation saying that Japan was going to need to bring itself into the future, into the modern age. To do that it was going to have to adopt a modern European language as its second language and start promulgating all its laws in that language, its education system in that language and so on. And there was no doubt that it was English he had in mind.

But unquestionably, the huge growth in the use of English by non native speakers has been over the past fifty years. **David Crystal**:

I think that what's happened essentially in the last half of the twentieth century is that many countries have started to want to talk to each other in ways that they hadn't done previously. The United Nations, for example – created in the middle of the century with fifty or so nation members in the 1950s, now fifty years on it has 189 or so members and nearly four times the number of organisations now wanting to talk together, having international meetings and so on, needing a lingua franca. And this has been a significant development in the twentieth century and one that seems likely to continue.

The United Nations in session.

But what sort of English is this lingua franca? The English of all these international agencies is a far cry from the full-strength language of Charles Dickens or Herman Melville. It has a morphology and a syntax that resemble basic English, but inevitably loses much of the detail. Reflect for a moment on the problems that the English verb 'get' must pose for the international community: 'get out', 'get in', 'get under', 'get away', 'get under way', 'get away with', 'get by', 'get from', 'get even', 'get ugly', and so on and so on. It is obvious that compromises have to be made. Thus English as a lingua franca is useful, though problematic.

At the University of Illinois, Professor Braj Kachru has spent over thirty years wrestling with the issue of English as a world language. Born in Kashmir, India, Kachru grew up speaking Kashmiri, though also possessing a command of Hindi and as his studies progressed, of English. Braj Kachru is one of the most distinguished observers of the English language outside Britain and America. In his classic book *The Alchemy of English* he developed the concept of the three concentric circles of English, which has been widely adopted by observers of the international English scene.

Kachru's 'Inner Circle' comprises the traditional English-speaking territories, having English as their mother tongue, in other words the UK, USA, Canada, Australia and New Zealand. Doing the sums, the total of core English speakers in the world is no more than 380 million. Set alongside that the one billion or more who have Mandarin Chinese as their first language, and one can only marvel at the power of English to dominate the world's preferred means of expression.

In Kachru's model, beyond these frontline English-using territories lies the 'Outer Circle' of nations where English has become sufficiently indigenised to account for

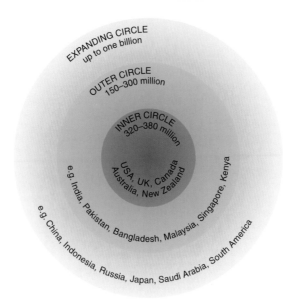

EXPANDING CIRCLE
up to one billion

OUTER CIRCLE
150–300 million

INNER CIRCLE
320–380 million

USA, UK, Canada
Australia, New Zealand

e.g. India, Pakistan, Bangladesh, Malaysia, Singapore, Kenya

e.g. China, Indonesia, Russia, Japan, Saudi Arabia, South America

many of the workings of the country – as we have seen in India, and also in places like Singapore. These nations account for some 150–300 million speakers.

Beyond the Outer Circle lies Professor Kachru's third zone of speakers, the 'Expanding Circle', in which English is the preferred adoptive medium of communication, with many practitioners in such territories as Russia and China. A maximum figure for these is, according to Kachru, one billion. David Graddol estimates that within fifty years the total will have reached 1.3 billion, and that figure only includes those who use English in a competent and regular manner; many more millions will have an approximate working knowledge of the language in which they can make rudimentary efforts.

Add up the figures and it soon becomes obvious that English as used by those who have adopted it as a second or third language has far greater currency than amongst those for whom it is the mother tongue, the 'proprietors' of English, as it were. All of which prompts the question: whose language is it anyway? English is like a tree, says **Braj Kachru**, akin to the banyan tree, with a central trunk – British English – and many branches looping out and coming back to earth to form new, powerful trunks.

People see English as a sort of 'Speaking Tree' – the Waqwaq tree of Indian mythology – and if in mythology this trunk of the tree created a feeling of awe, people also despised it. But people loved the branches. The branches used to sing songs of the Sun and Moon and charming and beautiful women, and that's how the branches of English are thriving

Professor Braj Kachru's three concentric circles of English.

around the world. But there still is suspicion of the trunk. There is suspicion about what are the motives of Britain. They sometimes associate the British Council with it. The motives of America, the motives of the publishing industry and the media, those too are suspect.

But language is a tool and it is flourishing. For example, in recent years the creativity in English, in fiction and poetry and other genres, is flourishing in South Asia, and you will repeatedly hear about that. These are being discussed in the mainstream media now. So I feel really that there is this sweet and sour feeling.

For many users of English who inhabit Kachru's Expanding Circle of acquired, utilitarian English, the socio-political dimension and the colonial and cultural baggage are not significant issues. This English is merely a tool, a means of reaching as wide and as diverse a community as possible. Non-governmental organisations (NGOs) belong in the main to this category, as do those who use English as a lingua franca for trade and international discourse. For these users, though, a stripped-down language shorn of its cultural baggage is the norm. Here the English is only as good as the user's acquired level, and it is not uncommon for apparently non-standard expressions and images to disrupt the flow of meaning.

At its most extreme, this can inhibit the central purpose of the communication, namely clear expression and understanding. Take this example written by a highly articulate English-speaking Belgian broadcaster, using his acquired English to address an international community (of radio documentarists) of whom perhaps only 30 per cent inhabit Kachru's Inner Circle of native speakers. I have underlined the deviations from standard British English.

'Last monday I had the pleasure to assist to a challenging meeting … in Paris. Theme of the evening : the position of the radio-author faced to the turmoil of changes in the program [=programming] and production policy of public radio. Before an audience of some 120 authors [=programme producers], editors, actors, sound engineers and composers 6 European feature makers were invited to expose their views on the matter. In spite of the hard times we face – and the not always positive conjuncture concerning author's radio – we never were challenged by so many colloquia, seminars, competitions, festivals and workshops as nowadays.

And we have to face reality: We will have to break out of what was once – at least for some of us – a splendid isolation. We left the comfortzone now. And our concern with what brews and simmers in society is an indefinable surplus also in today's radio …'

Taken overall, the meaning is reasonably clear, though the use of imagery and metaphors that seem unusual to a native English speaker does disrupt real understanding – just what is he talking about? Thus, for those for whom English is a purely acquired means of expression, lack of competency can inhibit communication just as much as the excessive use by mother-tongue speakers of locally-flavoured images and expressions.

However, if the meaning remains clear and it is only the form that is unconventional or 'non-standard', then maybe other rules apply – or will in the future. **David Graddol** on a topical dilemma:

The reality is that some new pattern of usage is emerging which doesn't look to native speakers for a model of correctness. In Europe, where European institutions are increasingly publishing material in English, they are not just translating material into English but finding that nationals of other countries are producing material in English, and the Translation Bureau at the European Commission is now faced with the problem of what to do with this. Do we actually turn it into native-speaker English or do we accept that there is emerging here a different kind of English, a kind of Euro-English with different usages, different kinds of syntax, different meanings attached to these words?

In this new world of the Euro-legislators on language, 'normal' rules no longer apply. This is the world of Euro-speak, which, though often maligned as meaningless and deriving more from bureaucracy than real life, nonetheless is having an insidious effect on English, as **David Graddol** has noticed.

For example, documentation coming out of Europe often uses English-looking words, but with senses that are more like the French. And I'm thinking here of key words like 'federal', 'subsidiarity', 'community' – these all have meanings which are closer to the French than to the Anglo-Saxon meaning. Another example is some words that are being used by Europeans in English that don't seem to have any existence in British English. In German English, for example, if you're on a Lufthansa flight you'll probably be told to 'Turn your handies off' as you take off – and a 'handy' is a hand phone, a mobile phone. The first time a native speaker hears that word they think 'What on earth is a "handy"?' But the Germans imagine that that is the word that we normally use.

And when setting up the visual element for a lecture in the heart of Europe, David Graddol recently found himself invited to connect his computer to a 'beamer'. This, it seems, is now accepted Euro-English for a projector – a claim that will undoubtedly be hotly contested by the average Brit-in-the-street for whom a 'beamer' is the popular way of referring to an expensive German motor vehicle. Which 'beamer' will end up on top? In the long run it does not matter too much. Each will have its own area of acceptance, and there are few circumstances in which the two homophones (words which sound the same) could cause confusion ('He put his beamer in his beamer'?).

In Sydney, I met **Dr Pam Peters** of Macquarie University who has made a particular study of English as a global means of expression. For a number of years her Langscape survey has charted the variation in customary spellings and usage of English across the world. And in 2001 her annual language conference, the Style Council, debated the issues surrounding the acquisition and use of English as a means of expression for the whole world. I put it to Dr Peters that 'deracinated' forms, such as the example from Belgium, could present as many difficulties as solutions – context is, indeed, all.

It's exactly those things that, as soon as we make our discourse connect with our surroundings, as soon as we want to give it life and vitality, we're going to pull in what is of the moment around us. The last thing you want to reel in then is the kind of abstract academic language that is genuinely international. And indeed it's very easy to publish an international academic paper because the conceptual notions are genuinely international. But when you want to talk and even to write in a local context, our local papers – any newspaper – are inclined to want to play up what are the events in the neighbourhood. And there too, in the written form as well as in speech, the newspaper will be highlighting local terminology to show that it's coming to grips with what's going on around it. So that one is I think always going to be a problem.

However, by the same token, the use of local non-standard forms to express globally applicable notions can be seen by passionate defenders of language as a threat.

I do see slightly more hope at the level of things like word forms – whether you say 'sailboat' or 'sailing-boat', whether you see 'defence' spelt with an 's' or a 'c' – in that these are matters of regularity within the language. And here I think people need not feel they have such a stake in whether it's British or American spelling. Second language users, who have no stake at all in this kind of thing, can more easily arbitrate in a way, participate in any kind of international discussion, because their views are less coloured.

For native speakers, on the other hand, the choice of a spelling often connects with their national identity or political affiliations. So here in Australia there's very commonly a problem for people over even whether you spell 'colour' C-O-L-O-R or C-O-L-O-U-R. And the angst that some people feel about American pressures in the region, or their economic and cultural hegemony, means that they therefore distance themselves from any kind of visible signs of Americanness.

I know this is true in Canada too, where there's an awful battle being fought out in places like Toronto as to whether you could dare to use American spellings – they're, as it were, your neighbours and far too close for comfort, if you're a Canadian. And so people – I think not entirely rationally – then want to reject American forms of the English language that we share with them, even if those American forms are actually more regular and would be easier for our children to learn as well as second-language users of the language.

So, in effect, what Dr Peters is saying is that those English speakers for whom it is a second or third language, without the cultural baggage of native speakers, may be the new rule-makers, the gatekeepers of world English. This is a view firmly subscribed to by a pair of cutting-edge research linguists working together in London and Vienna.

Dr Jennifer Jenkins of King's College, University of London, has for some time been engaged on a major study with Barbara Seidlhofer of what she refers to as ELF – English as a lingua franca. She says that on the basis of sheer weight of numbers alone, the second-language English users – L2 speakers – will determine the future shape of the language. Jenkins sees the old native varieties as the foundations of a great house, rising higher and higher as more floors (in the shape of different styles of usage of the language) are added. She considers these new and non-standard varieties will help shore up the old creaking structure with their adaptable, regularised forms and 'go anywhere' phraseology. For example:

We 'talk about' something and we 'discuss' something. Virtually all L2 speakers 'discuss about' something – I'm sure that's going to come in very quickly even among native speakers. There's the tag expression 'how can I say?' – I've heard that a lot among a whole range of L2 speakers. These processes of 'regularisation' go on naturally in language and in the past it has been the native speakers who have been 'allowed' to make them. Increasingly it's going to be the non native speakers who make them.

And native speakers will have to follow suit! But as the world of English becomes ever more extended, so will its need and its capacity to form locally distinct varieties – dialects if you like – that suit local needs. It is a process already well under way, according to **David Crystal**.

On the one hand there is standard English, which exists through the medium of print very largely around the newspapers and the textbooks of the world, and that is not likely to change. The dialect of those people who speak standard English is so firmly entrenched amongst the educated people in the world that I doubt that's going to change in the foreseeable future. But at grass-roots level some amazing things are happening, producing varieties of English that are quite unlike anything that we've heard of previously, and so different from standard English that sometimes it is virtually impossible to understand what's going on. If you listen to somebody speaking 'Singlish' in Singapore, which is a mixture of English and Chinese, then because it is a mixture of the two languages, only if you know both are you likely to understand it.

When I was last in Singapore I did not understand some of the 'English' that people were speaking around me. And that's the point, that as English develops in the twenty-first century we're going to see an increasing multi-dialectalisation of it. We're going to need to become multilingual in it, those of us who travel the world, if we're going to communicate with everybody. But nobody will be able to do that, and we'll all end up speaking just one or two dialects of an increasingly complex English world scene.

It's only the same thing happening on the world scale as has always happened on a national scale. We're used to national accents and dialects – we're not used to international accents and dialects. It's the same process, the process that drives an accent or dialect into existence is the need for identity.

Standard languages give you guaranteed intelligibility, local accents and dialects give you identity, and at a world level this is exactly what's happening. What you're going to get is Swedish English, Netherlands English, Brazilian English – in other words, people from these foreign languages of the world who are speaking their English in a local way, with the influence of their mother tongues shaping the language in fresh directions.

As David Crystal says, the very localised nature of these new regional 'dialects' can present problems of intelligibility to native English users such as himself. As part of her research, **Jennifer Jenkins** has been focusing on the phonology – the pronunciation – of English of those for whom it is not the mother tongue. According to her findings, many (though not all) consonants are very important to the intelligibility of English.

A Korean who talked about 'pailing' his driving test instead of 'failing' it, now that caused a lot of problems – the 'p' instead of the 'f'. And the other thing that mattered very much was groups of consonants, so you get a Taiwanese who talks about a 'poduk' instead of a 'product' – especially at the beginnings of words the 'pr' was very important. If you ask people where they eat hamburgers and chips and they say 'Madonul', that's very difficult for many L2 speakers to understand. Also the difference between long and short vowel sounds – the 'i' sound in 'live' compared with the long 'ee' in 'leave'. At least for the moment that caused a lot of miscommunication.

From her work for the Vienna-Oxford corpus, Jenkins's colleague Barbara Seidlhofer has undertaken to identify elements that native speakers would consider 'incorrect', yet which result in no miscommunication. One of the most obviously 'wrong' elements for a native speaker – common among L2s – is missing off the third person 's', as in 'I like', 'you like', 'he like'. **Jennifer Jenkins**:

They're also missing out a lot of the articles, so something like 'Could you show me book?' doesn't seem to cause problems. 'Who' and 'which' – 'the person which', 'the book who' – are other typical cases that seem not to matter. And using the base form of the verb is another typical example, so 'I look forward to seeing you' becomes 'I look forward to see you'.

There is also a movement towards a universal question tag of the 'isn't it?' variety.

The tag system in English, 'have you?', 'haven't you?', 'could you?', 'couldn't you?', 'won't you?', 'didn't you?', is horrendously complicated and it's not very helpful for meaning. There are a number of possibilities – in Spain they often just say '¿no?', or there's the French 'non?'. Germans often use 'oder', you've got French 'n'est-ce pas?', and Professor David Crystal has suggested it might end up as 'nesspa?' as the universal tag. You've got 'isn't it?' in Sri Lanka and 'is it?' in Singapore. Now any of those could end up as being a universal question tag. We don't know which one it'll be.

What all these commentators – Graddol, Crystal and Jenkins – agree on is that the shape of English to come will to a large extent, at least on a global level, be legislated by non native speakers. Many of the elements will eventually be codified as ELF – English as a lingua franca –and native speakers will have to learn these if they want to speak internationally. That is not to say, however, that native varieties are entirely losing their status, according to **David Graddol**. Indeed ...

Our knowledge of English as native speakers is looked towards with envy by many other learners of English round the world, and native speakers are still regarded by very many people as the 'gold standard' internationally, but in many ways that's looking back to some kind of golden past.

Over the past ten or twenty years it has been the vision of a sort of 'golden future' that has obsessed technologically literate analysts, researchers and crystal-ball gazers in the world of socio-linguistics. The great light illuminating this future has been the internet. The net's astonishing growth, from a small-scale tool for academic information exchange in the 1980s to the huge engine for the promulgation of information, images and sound that we know today, has touched every part of the globe. The language in which that engine has operated up to now has very largely been English – and, conventionally, American English.

The received wisdom was simply this: the internet works in English; to get anywhere on the net you have to be able to understand and express yourself in English. Therefore English suddenly takes on the status of a vital – and fashionable – tool for using, interpreting and appreciating the net. **David Crystal**, who has made an in-depth study of the new medium, charts its progress – downwards:

When the internet started it was of course 100 per cent English because of where it came from, but since the late 1980s that status has started to fall away. By 1995 it was down to about 80 per cent presence of English on the internet, and the current figures for 2001 are that it is hovering somewhere between 60 per cent and 70 per cent, with a significant drop likely over the next four or five years. There are at least 1,500 languages present on the internet now and that figure is likely to increase. But will that affect the permanent presence of English? Of course not. English is the dominant presence and will remain so.

With a keen eye for historical parallels, **David Graddol** enters a caveat:

The internet has in the past twenty years been a very important factor in the spread and adoption of English – but I think it's only a very passing phase. It's also a phase that

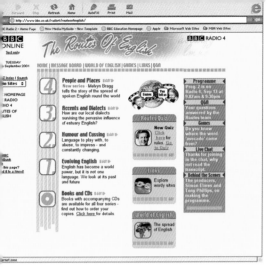

started much longer ago with the spread of the telegraph in the late nineteenth century. That was the technology that first wired the world and first had English humming down the wires. But now the biggest story is not the use of English on the internet but the use on it of languages other than English. And we're seeing the emergence of a technology that is very supportive of multilingualism and local languages and local cultures and which is being used more and more by people who do not speak English as their first language.

From the albeit highly subjective and limited evidence of my research for this book in India, the manner in which the internet is currently being used in the subcontinent supports Dr Graddol's claim. Natish Jain, who runs a string of internet parlours in Calcutta, says that the language overwhelmingly preferred for sending e-mails is English, although it is often blended with a second local language such as Hindi or Bengali. Thus the 'internet effect' appears not simply to be spreading the influence of English but also to be enhancing the regionalisation of it that David Crystal referred to.

At the Style Council in Sydney, the keynote conference speech was given by the acknowledged world expert on English as a global language, **Professor Edgar Schneider** of Regensburg University in Germany. Professor Schneider gave his address, naturally, in English. But which English? Listening closely, I noticed that Professor Schneider's English had a great degree of fluency, though still retaining a light touch of German accent, as well as the pronounced 'r' following a vowel sound that is typical of standard American.

In our school system we used to be taught British English, and then increasingly nowadays you get the impact of American forms from various sources, mostly popular culture, music, that kind of thing. As a scholar you can spend some time in the States and you end up with a sort of mixed variety, I guess. That's what you get increasingly in societies with high levels of migration.

It depends on what you use the language for – that probably is the crucial point. With someone like me who's a second-language user, it's not really that much a question of expressing identities. When I come to Australia and speak to Australians, I tend to drop some of the post-vocalic 'r's with my strongly American-accented type of speech. I usually have to adjust because I find Australians sympathetic and that's the way you go along.

So, at least when an L2 user addresses native speakers, he is heard to be making concessions to accommodate local prejudices, local tastes and local cultural values. So what price 'neutral' English?

If it's an expression of an identity then I think there is always the strong tendency for differences to be retained because you do express who you are, who you want to be, where you come across, by means of language. That seems to be the cheapest, the easiest possible way of expressing identities. Language is not just about carrying information. It's certainly about communicating – and that also means communicating hidden identities under the surface, and that goes through things like accents and varieties and so on. That's what you really identify with.

The world of English today lies a very long way beyond the Lincolnshire lanes of the future settlers of Plymouth, Massachusetts, or the Bristol streets trodden by John Cadman before he was transported to a new life in New South Wales. Wherever it has gone, English has changed, adapted and adopted a shape that suits its purpose. In many ways, that is its strength and its value: to accommodate, flex and make itself work for those who adopt it.

By way of conclusion, a further word about one of the newest and most interesting arenas where English is breaking new ground as a means of everyday expression. In the former British colony of Singapore, English has remained, as in India, the language of government and administration. In the media and education, likewise, English has a prominent place. Having already achieved a considerable level of usage amongst the population, the language is now set, according to **Edgar Schneider**, to achieve an even greater level of importance.

Singapore seems to be a very unique case. Of all the countries to which English has been transported, at least those where there's a strong majority of the indigenous people, in Singapore the local people – Chinese, Malay, Tamils and so on – are still adopting English as their first language, as their native language, as far as we can tell. And increasingly so.

There's an enormous percentage of the population where English is used as the family language because the parents presumably come from varying linguistic backgrounds. So the children grow up with English as their L1 [native language]. And that has to do with questions of identity as well because in Singapore it's English that is seen as a carrier of a new national identity. So I would dare to predict that in the long run Singapore might really be a more or less English-speaking country. I'd say in about 200 years – but I'm glad nobody can prove me wrong in that!

Acknowledgements

Sincere thanks to everyone who made this final series and book of *The Routes of English* possible, including:
Prof William Labov, University of Pennsylvania
Dr Anna Celia Zentella, New York City University
Bill Bryson
Scott Attwood
Betty Cortina, *Latina* magazine
Amit Chaudhuri
Prof Sukanta Chaudhuri, Jadavpur University
Prof Raja Ram Mehrotra, Banaras University
Dr Samita Sen, Calcutta University
Kushal Biswas
The students of La Martiniere College for Girls, Calcutta
Dr Hubert Devenish, University of the West Indies
Peter Roberts, University of the West Indies
Richard Allsopp, Caribbean Lexicography Project
Derek Walcott
Joan Andrea Hutchinson
Professor Frank Clarke, Macquarie University, Sydney
Dr David Blair, Dean of Humanities, Macquarie University, Sydney
Dr Kate Burridge, La Trobe University, Melbourne
Dr Susan Butler, Executive Editor, *The Macquarie Dictionary*
Bruce Moore, Editor, *The Australian National Dictionary*
The people of Bathurst, New South Wales
Albie Sachs
John Kani
Professor Raj Mesthrie, University of Cape Town
Penny Silva, Deputy Editor, *Oxford English Dictionary*
Professor David Crystal
Dr Jennifer Jenkins, King's College, University of London
Dr David Graddol
Dr Pam Peters, Macquarie University, Sydney
Professor Edgar Schneider, Regensburg University

Huge thanks of course to BBC colleagues without whom none of this would have happened at all, especially Helen Boaden, Controller Radio 4, producer Tony Phillips, researcher Sarah Bowen and Broadcast Assistant Christine Saunders. For support and the odd glass of wine when things looked black, Richard Bannerman, Editor, Documentaries, and my wife Liz, who put up with me disappearing to the other side of the world.

Picture credits

AKG: front cover, pp. 26, 92
Associated Press: p. 80
Norman Barnfather: p. 44
BBC: Foreword, Introduction, p.115, back cover
British Library: p. 86
Simon Elmes: pp. 25, 29, 37, 39, 59, 61, 64, 70, 76
Hulton Getty: pp. 23, 32, 79, 97, 102
ImageState: pp. 1, 17, 41
Janet Marc: p. 104
Mary Evans Picture Library: pp. 4, 11, 12, 15, 34, 47, 62, 66, 75, 83
PA Photos: pp. 99, 117
Tony Phillips: pp. 3, 21, 48, 50, 81, 89
Carol Stanley: pp. 6, 9, 109
CD cover, p. 56, courtesy of Kaiso Records, London (020 7368 3393)

The Routes of English website:
www.bbc.co.uk/radio4/routesofenglish